Preparing Yourself to Succeed in College:

A Professor's Guide to Choosing a College and Thriving in Your First Year

William Pizio, Ph.D.

Printed in the United States of America
A 2 Z Press LLC
PO Box 582
Deleon Springs, FL 32130
terriesizemorestoryteller.com
terriesizemorestoryteller@gmailcom
386-681-7402

ISBN: 978-1-946908-91-9

ACKNOWLEDGMENTS

It is difficult to put into words how much I could possibly appreciate the wonderful people in my life who helped me with this book.

Trying to remember all the advice I have given over my twenty-three years of teaching would be impossible if not for my wife, Leanne. She has given me more support than I could possibly express in words. Her advice when writing this book was honest, critical, and unbelievably constructive. She made me a better writer and for all of that, I am beyond grateful. She also illustrated the cover, just so you know. Thank you, my wife. Thank you.

There were others who made this process a great one. Teri Sizemore, my publisher, was always there with her wisdom and experience in the publishing world. Learning difference expert Georgian Bogdean was instrumental with that chapter. Janet Schaefer and Susan Dolan were extraordinary proofreaders. I also wanted to give credit to the students who read various parts of the manuscript and told me when I got it right and more importantly, when I got it wrong! Rebekah Langston, Sabrina Farah and Lotty Hennessy, I have learned a great deal from all of you. A special thanks goes to you, Chickweed. Thank you for the gift of your fifteen years.

To all students who read on: I hope this book helps you, even if it is just a little.

TABLE OF CONTENTS

Introduction to the Book

A Professor's Perspective

I was a terrible high school student! I was also a terrible freshman and sophomore in college. I cared less than I should have and I was happy to just get by. It was not until my junior year that I felt like 'I got it.' I figured out what I wanted to be and how I needed to get there. It took me that long to figure it out and it was a long road for both my parents and me! I want this book to help you to avoid taking the same road I did!

What is college really like? How do I pick the right college for me? What questions should I ask when I visit colleges and who should I talk to? What is my first year going to be like? How much freedom will I have? Where should I study? How long should I study?

What techniques help me learn the best? How can I successfully balance my academics and social life? How can professors help me? What resources does my college have to offer and how can I best utilize those resources? What do I want to do with my life and do I really have to decide when I am seventeen or eighteen years old?

These are just a few of the questions that are probably swirling around in your mind. As your search for the right college begins, you are going to be bombarded with information from all sides. High school guidance counselors have years of experience answering questions. College admissions counselors help future students decide by speaking to the benefits of their specific college and how that college would be the best fit for them. Parents impart wisdom from their experiences. Many fine scholars have also written books and guides that give valuable information. Make no mistake, a high school student who is contemplating college should take full advantage of all these.

As talented and valuable as these resources are, there is an important missing piece. Where do college professors come in to play? Should college professors come in to play? The answer is clearly yes. As faculty, we have a perspective unlike any of the other resources available to high school students. We have years of experience teaching first year students and we have seen many before you come and go. With all different kinds of students and learners, we have seen what works and what does not. Based on that experience, we clearly know how to be a successful student and that comes from a much different perspective than the other people you are getting good advice from.

We meet with prospective and current students often and guide them to ask questions they might not think to ask. We speak with parents about their children. We also communicate with other members of our college, both faculty and staff, when academic, social, or emotional concerns arise with students. This gives us a unique perspective on college that no one else can have. In short, we are an incredibly underutilized resource for those seeking guidance on choosing a college and success in college once they arrive.

While prospective students might have the opportunity to interview or briefly speak with a faculty member during their campus visits, those visits usually consist of the student asking questions about the college in general or the specific major or department that interests them. It is rare that a professor is given the full opportunity to help that high school student make important college choices.

Professors are wonderfully suited to help guide the student through their college career once enrolled. While students do learn how to become college students, many do it on their own and do it by observing other students. While that may work in some cases, we know how to succeed as students because we are the ones teaching them. In years of teaching, experienced faculty see thousands and thousands of students come through and there is no one better prepared to help teach students (prospective and enrolled) *how* to be a successful college student.

Learning to be a Successful College Student and Your Two Educations

It takes work. Being a successful college student takes work. I am talking about more than just the content of your classes. I am talking about how to succeed in the transition to college, academics, administrative duties, and in social life. You can get help in many places but professors have the experience to help you understand this process. Personally, I feel that if you do not pay attention to the transition, you will not really learn how to be a successful college student until the middle of your sophomore year. Sometimes, this process can be painful and low grades may result. Other times, you may receive exceptional grades because of incessant studying but miss out on the other side of college. In short, you must learn how to navigate college and everything that comes with it and this book seeks to help you do just that.

At a four-year institution where you will live on campus, the tuition that you pay is for two separate and distinct educations. The first education is the one you receive in the classroom. You delve into your major and colleges will require you to take a variety of classes in different disciplines to make you better rounded. Whether classes in the sciences, foreign languages, or humanities, to name a few, you will take classes that fit 'general education' requirements. Again, their goal is to make you a better-rounded, educated person who can be a functioning member of society. You can be the smartest astrophysicist in the world but if you cannot have an educated discussion with another person on a subject not related to astrophysics, then the college is not doing their job.

The second education you receive at college revolves around the social aspect. Few speak directly to the non-academic side of college but it is an incredibly important part where learning clearly takes place. In my opinion, you will learn as much living in the residence halls as you will in your classes. You will learn everything from conflict resolution and diversity training to multi-cultural training and interpersonal communications. You will learn how to navigate relationships and understand how to live and communicate with people who have very different viewpoints and backgrounds. You might begin your first adult relationship. For the first time, you might be in or see inter-racial or homosexual relationships. You might be in or see friends in unhealthy and potentially damaging relationships. What you learn from this part of your education is absolutely invaluable.

This Book

This is precisely the reason I am writing this book. If you think about all of the available resources for prospective and current college students, professors sadly do not generally make the top five when in fact, they should. I feel that as faculty, our talents are totally underutilized. We are the ones who are there to help guide you throughout your time at college. We are the ones who have communicated with, taught, and have learned from thousands of college students before you. We are the ones who are *always* the most experienced at college. We have gone to college and as professors; we have seen it all and have a wealth of knowledge to share

As such, this book is written for two specific audiences. The first is the high school student who is beginning to think about college. The second is the incoming first year college student. If parents can benefit from this as well, then all the better. On this road to becoming a college student and then becoming a successful college student, college professors have a perspective on college that is utterly unique.

In the following pages, this book will talk about these things. My goal is to help you pick your college by having everything you need to make an informed choice. My goal is to give you techniques you can use that will make your life in college much easier. My goal is for you to start using these techniques now. I want you to enjoy *all* of your college experiences and if this book can help ease some of your worries and help you save time with your tasks, then I have succeeded.

Everyone Can Succeed In College

I strongly believe that every single person can succeed in college and you are included! You could be the smartest person on the block or the one that struggles academically. Neither of these types of students can guarantee that they will succeed in college. The brilliant person may get wonderful grades but may be stressed out all of the time and have a less robust social life. The student who struggles academically may not avail themselves of all the support mechanisms a college has to offer – and they do offer! Even those with learning differences can easily succeed in college with the right guidance and the willingness to ask for help.

There is another type of student who may greatly benefit from this book. There are many students who come to college who have high levels of anxiety, whether social or academic. I am not a psychiatrist and do not pretend to be one but I do know that the skills I work to teach you in this book can reduce your stress and anxiety levels. If you can approach and complete tasks in the most efficient way possible, how cannot that reduce your anxiety levels? During the course of this book, I will have some direct information for students with high anxiety but even when I am not referring directly to those types of students, the advice I give can help reduce stress levels. You just have to try what I advise and let it work for you or modify it so it works for you.

What's in this Book that Can Help You

In this book, I have tried to think of every piece of advice I have given in my over twenty years of college teaching.

The Search

I speak to the college search and how to be fully informed about the colleges you are thinking of attending. I try to give you the right questions to ask and the right things to do when you visit colleges (hopefully you will visit your top choices twice). I ask you to go out of the normal channels to get more information. For example, I want you to speak to other students, go to the professors in the department you plan to major in and eat in the cafeteria with students who attend that college. For you to be fully informed and get all the information for your decision about a college, you must go beyond what the college chooses to tell you and show you.

Let me be clear: With decreasing enrollments, colleges try to sell themselves. They will send information and work to woo the prospective student to attend. If you are a high school student near the higher end of your class, then the sales pitches become even more intrusive, in both frequency and level of invasiveness. If you have been in this position before, you understand. If you have not experienced this yet, I promise you will. I just want you to be able to move beyond the sales pitch and get the truest sense of what each college is really like.

Differences Between High School and College

The third chapter looks at the differences between high school and college to give you an idea before you walk in the door. In this chapter, my goal is to make you better prepared for what you are going to face academically. The differences may be stark and shocking to you and knowing what to expect can make all the difference.

Your First Semester

The next chapters guide you through orientations and your first semester. The transition will be difficult and stress can manifest itself in many ways. You may be homesick or you may be overly social. You may simply not do your work and go to class (yes, this happens quite a bit with first year students) or you may be incredibly stressed out. There are many other ways your stress over this transition can show and these chapters are meant to both prepare you for those stress levels and give you tools to manage and push past them.

Being an Efficient and Effective Student

Chapters 6 and 7 are all about the way to tackle the tasks you will encounter at college, both academic and administrative. Your job will be to succeed academically but there are so many tools you need to have that can guide you toward success. I will give study and test taking skills but I will also give advice on how to manage your time and get the classes that you need and want. Remember, I am not a college administrator. I am a college professor who (I feel) has seen it all. I am also the type of person who works incredibly hard to be efficient because the one enemy of college professors is hours in the day. There are tasks that I do, I have received advice from other faculty, and that is what these two chapters are all about.

Advice for Students with Learning Differences

Having a learning difference can add additional stress to a college student's academic and social life but colleges are there to help. Their help may not be the same type of help you received in your schooling to now and knowing those differences about what college can and must offer is important. It is crucial that you are aware of the laws and how your educational success is guided by a different law than the one that guides you during high school. I will also give some skills to help you succeed. That advice may include things you have heard before but I work to focus on what I have seen work in my capacity as a professor.

A Chapter for your Parents (and you)

Parents are your supporters, administrators, and cheerleaders. They help guide your college search process. They want to help but in many cases, they will want to take control of the college search process if they do not feel that you are active enough. While actually in college, they want to help you succeed.

In the end, however, it is your education and you have to take control. I am not saying that you should shut your parents out but your college is there for you to control. Let them guide and allow them to be a sounding board but know that it is your education.

This chapter introduces several topics and then gives advice for both you and your parents on each topic.

Success Revisited

I absolutely believe you can succeed at college and my sole goal writing this book is to facilitate that success. Finding the right college is the first step toward that success. The second part of the equation is to offer strategies to ease your transition during your first semester. Lastly, you want to be efficient in the academic and administrative tasks you will have to complete throughout your college career. If you take some or all of my advice in this book, I can guarantee that you will be a better college student and your chances of success will increase dramatically.

Do not be worried if you do not know your true path yet. Personally, I do not feel that a college freshman should choose what they want to do with their life when they are 18 years old. College is a time to start figuring your life out. Once you get to college, then you start to grow and experiment with classes. By doing this, you will start narrowing the ideas of what you want to do with your life.

Please use your professors. We are the ones who will be your teachers, mentors and advisors. We will meet you in our offices and talk on the phone with you. We have likely seen just about everything and can help. Come to us and let us help you succeed. I know you can do it!

So, read on and have fun. You can succeed in college and I strongly believe every single student can. Let me try to make it easier for you!

Choosing a College – Initial Research

Introduction

Early on in high school, you likely encountered college information overload from all conceivable angles. Your guidance counselor has probably talked about the SAT as well as possible career and college opportunities. I am sure your parents have spoken to you about college and have strongly encouraged you to engage in extra-curricular activities to bolster your applications. If they have not already, colleges will begin to be in contact if you show even the slightest interest (i.e. filling out a form on their website). Before anything else, let me make one thing very clear: Colleges are businesses and will market directly to you to gain your business. Think about it. If they spend $500 in marketing materials and personnel time and you attend, the payback the college gets is huge. A

13

hundred thousand dollars in payback if you choose to attend and stay all four years is not unheard of. That is a serious profit. Please just keep this in mind when you start to show interest and begin to contact colleges.

Choosing a college to attend is complicated. Some high school students will have a single college they want to attend and have already decided on a major. Others, and more likely the most of you, will still be in the decision phase in one or both areas. *This is normal and you are not alone!* Therefore, finding a college where you are a good fit can be difficult and this may stem from the lack of information about a specific college or university.

When deciding which colleges you want to visit and tour, there are several important factors that you must consider and activities you must undertake to be able to make an informed choice (on a side note, I chose my first college because I liked the way the campus looked. This was not a good choice and I learned that the hard way). Because traveling to several colleges is a time consuming and expensive endeavor, it is important to narrow down your choices before you visit. Below you will find recommendations for digging into your college research and a list of considerations to take into account. The list may not have all the factors that are important to you but will give you an idea of things to think about when choosing a school.

You can also find variations of this list on many webpages and publications out there. Almost all of the ones you find online will be different and are based on the focus and background of the author. Look at as many lists as you can because one list will never have every single factor that is important to you. Getting as much information from different sources as you can makes your decision making process a smart one. Given that, this book guides these decisions from a professor's perspective, I wanted to give advice on *how* to research and then *what* to research (the list). The list of factors in this chapter will be loosely ordered by what a faculty member would likely find to be most important.

Research, Research, Research

Research, Research, Research. Prior to any college visits, you will need to complete research on the schools you are thinking about attending. You would not go into the SAT or a final exam without studying so you should not make the decision to go to college without doing your homework. While the college visit is a crucial piece to this puzzle, what you do prior to your visits is equally important.

You could certainly read profiles of various colleges online or in a book and learn quite a bit about each of them (i.e. Fiske Guide, Princeton Review, Colleges that Change Lives, U.S News and World Report, Barron's Profiles of American Colleges). You will get all the statistics, learn about the student body and the majors offered, job placement rates, and tuition information. Depending on the source you look at, there is much more information you could obtain.

The problem that arises with the beginning of your college research is that you are likely getting very generic information about the schools and the more colleges you look at, the more likely you will be to see the same or similar information. The homework analogy mentioned above also fits here. Why would you find ten sources that tell you exactly the same piece of information for your paper or assignment? The answer is: you would not. You work to use different sources to add to or augment the information you already have.

The same holds true for this type of research. I suggest that you find enough generic information to allow you to get a good view of the colleges you are looking at. Then the important work begins. This is the point where you should get as much information as you can while focusing on *the factors that are important to you*. When reading the list of different factors below, rank them in relation to importance for you and use them to help determine which schools are at the top of your list and which schools are not. I suggest you work through your factors in a step-wise manner rather than as a single decision. By step-wise, I mean that you should find the most important factor, limit your search to those colleges that meet that specific criteria, and make a list of the colleges that have made the cut. Then start researching the second most important factor but *only* research that factor with the schools from that made the first cut (in other words, don't start from scratch). Then continue in this manner until you have a handful of colleges that you would definitely attend if you were accepted.

For example, if you have your heart set on certain size schools in a certain area of the country, and then narrow your search to that. If you have financial constraints, take the schools from the first list and research tuition only on those schools (keeping in mind that it is unlikely that you will pay the sticker price). Then keep going in this manner. The list will become much more manageable as you move on. At the absolute least, the schools at the top of your list <u>should have the major you intend to declare</u>. You would be surprised by the number of students who choose to attend a college that does not have the major they want. Even though many students also change majors once they attend college for a year or two, it would be advisable to have an idea of what you will major in.

This process has several benefits compared to looking at all important factors for each school at the same time. First, this will make your research more efficient. The process of elimination is a process that you already engage in with your daily decisions. Let us say you want a burger for lunch. You start there and then think about places that you know have good burgers. Then you think about the time you have to eat and narrow your search to those that serve fast. Then you think about how far you want to drive, the quality of the burger, and the sides. This narrowing continues until you make your decision. Now, I am not saying that you should go through a 15-minute thought process before deciding on lunch. What I am saying is that you already use this process in your daily life and do so very quickly. The process of eliminating undesirable options is a very efficient way to narrow your choices (i.e. colleges).

Second, this process makes your research more manageable. If you attempt to look for all your priorities at the same time with all the schools you are interested in, your research will get confusing. Schools will start to blend in with each other because your list is not narrowed until all your research is complete. I will talk more about efficiency later but for now, this process will save you time and frustration.

Here is an example. Have you ever gotten into an argument with someone about a topic and within minutes, the subject has changed to different ones? By the time you are well into your discussion, the topic has completely changed and you never get to address your original concern or problem. If you are able to keep the discussion limited to your initial concern, you will have a much better chance of resolving whatever conflict you have. You can use that same focus when narrowing down your college search. In other words, focusing in on what you feel are the important qualities in a college allows you to stay focused and not get distracted by the sales pitch or other factors that aren't that important to you.

Rather than be overwhelmed and research in a dysfunctional manner, parallel thinking, the third benefit, can be very helpful. With your college decision, parallel thinking is where you assess all the colleges in relation to one factor. For example, if you are examining location or proximity to home, you rank all the colleges you are looking at in regard to only that factor. You certainly would not want to go through this process with every single school you are looking at but once you narrow it down a bit, this process works wonders. Just as when you are resolving conflicts, staying on task with a specific topic or factor will help keep you focused.

If you are reading closely, you will have noticed that I keep referring to the work that *you* need to be doing. This is the next four years of your life and the decision is big. Please ask your parents questions and utilize them as sounding boards but this is your work, not theirs. In my experience, parents want to take the lead and do some, if not all, of the work for you. It is easier for you and they get to take care of you in the same way they have been doing for eighteen years. Avoid this at all cost because once you go away to college - that will end.

If you are not 'good at' administrative work because you have not had to do it, that is no excuse. Moreover, when you are at college, no one will be there to do that work except you. Whether it is small homework assignments, keeping a calendar or applying for next year's housing, it is time for you to take the lead. As director of my college's first year center, I cannot describe how many phone calls I received from parents asking questions for their children. Questions that you have about a college you are interested in should be asked by you and no one else. You will see that this will be the theme throughout this book. This is your education and transition to being an adult and you should be the one to do the legwork toward that goal.

Factors to Consider When Researching College

School Size

Some college students relish large school atmosphere and spirit. There is always something to do, somewhere to go, or a NCAA game being played. Others seek the more intimate learning experience of a smaller school. There are both benefits and drawbacks to large and small schools and this consideration is one that guides many high school students. It would be smart to tour schools of various sizes and in various locations (i.e. urban/rural) to get a feel for what works for you.

Small colleges will have more direct faculty interaction in and out of the classroom. Your professors will also be your advisors and will get to know whom you are and what you are looking for in classes and college as a whole. You will have much smaller classes and depending on the size of the school; there may even be no lecture halls or classrooms that fit over 30 or 40 students. Smaller schools also breed a more tight knit community in class, social organizations, and the college student political system.

Conversely, the facilities (sport, fitness, academic classrooms, etc.) may not be state of the art

19

and this will depend primarily on how much money the school has to spend on their facilities. The NCAA sports presence will not be that strong in Division II or III colleges, which are typically smaller than the larger Division I schools. Additionally, gossip travels fast in a small school depending on how small the school is and that may be too much like high school for you. Just for your information, there are several colleges in existence that have less than 200 students enrolled in them and if you were wondering, the largest school in the U.S. is currently the University of Central Florida with over 50,000 undergraduate students (Freidman, 2016).

The larger universities will have a wider variety of majors to choose from and more class offerings. Their faculty will be more famous (in college circles) and you will be learning from the professors and researchers that write the books in your major courses. They will also have stronger and more pronounced athletic programs and if you are looking for a strong sense of athletic school spirit, a larger school may be right for you. Larger colleges will also have a stronger variety of extracurricular activities.

Conversely, you will have much larger classes and graduate teaching assistants teach many. PhD students taught most of my freshman and sophomore courses in my major. While this may not necessarily be problematic, it is simply a factor to be considered. Students who arrive at the larger schools may also feel more overwhelmed due to the sheer size of the campus and all the people. Of the larger schools, Penn State is one of the biggest, covering approximately 8500 acres. Interestingly, the college in the United States that has the largest campus is Berry College in Georgia. They have only 2250 students but their campus is approximately 27,000 acres – that is 42 square miles (American School and University, n.d.).

Student to Faculty Ratio

Similar to the size of the school, student to faculty ratios vary quite a bit. Smaller liberal arts colleges will have a ratio of approximately 10-18 students for each faculty member. Larger universities will have a much larger student to faculty ratio but that number you see might be misleading. It is true that the lower level courses might have over 100 students (or more) at larger schools but as you move through your college major, you will find the upper level courses will have significantly fewer students in them. To move beyond that student to faculty ratio 'number,' go on to the websites of colleges you are interested in and find their course schedule pages to see what the maximum number of students for courses is as well as the actual enrollments for specific courses. It is especially important to do this for the major(s) you are considering. Note: This will also help you learn to navigate college websites and become efficient at navigating course schedule pages (something that you will need to learn – Chapter 7 will address this in more detail).

On the college's course schedule page, navigate to a subject or major you are interested in and when prompted, choose the semester the college is currently in. When you get there, you will want to find the actual enrollment (the number of students currently registered for the class) compared to the maximum enrollment (the maximum number of students who can enroll in the class). If you do this, make sure you scroll from the top to the bottom of the web pages since the introductory level courses will appear at the top of the webpage and the upper level courses will be toward the bottom of the webpage. The goal of this exercise is for you to have a good idea of how big the classes that you will be in are.

Course Availability and Your Potential Major

As noted above, learning to navigate a college's course schedule webpage(s) will be crucial once you are enrolled. In high school, however, you can still gain benefits. First off, navigate to each of your potential college's course schedule pages and find the major you think you will declare. Make sure you are looking at the semester the college is currently in. There are several things you want to look for:

> **The number of courses that are offered including the introductory courses.** You want to make sure there are enough introductory course offerings and that they are not full. You will also want to determine how many courses (in total) are being offered in your potential major.

> **The number of upper level required and elective courses that are offered.** Required and elective courses for a particular major usually can be found quite easily on that specific department's web page. Colleges that are having financial difficulties may be forced to offer fewer electives because faculty are forced to teach all required courses.

> **The maximum number of students that can enroll in the courses.** Are the classes large or small?

> **The number currently enrolled in the courses.** Will you be able to get into the classes or will they reach maximum capacity before you have a chance to register?

➤ **The times the courses are offered.** What is the ratio of day versus night course offerings?

➤ **Reserved spots for first year students, if any.** You may have a tough time finding classes and classes at preferred times since current students usually get to register before incoming first year students. If you cannot find this on the course schedule pages, you should ask at the tour or call the college's first year center and ask someone there.

You can and should do this with several potential majors in the colleges you are seriously considering. By spending the time here, you will get a great idea of how a college offers classes and how varied they are in relation to time, day and availability. If there are few course options (particularly elective courses), it may be worth an inquiry during your tour.

The Faculty

There are three general categories of faculty at colleges. The first category contains professors who are either tenured or tenure-track. These professors have gone through a rigorous national search and interview process and have terminal degrees in their field (the highest degree that can be obtained – usually a Ph.D.). They were hired because a search committee made up of several faculty members believed that they were the top of that particular applicant pool. These professors have also made a commitment to the particular college and have gone through (or are in the middle of) a series of rigorous reviews that assess their qualities (i.e. teaching, advising, professional scholarship, community service). When they get tenured (usually 6-

8 years after they get hired), it means that the college has examined that professor from several angles over several time periods and has determined that they deserve to have lifetime employment at that institution.

The second category of faculty is visiting lecturer or professor. They are full time but are temporary or contract employees. This usually means that the department had a faculty vacancy and for whatever reason, did not complete a national search. These faculty members may have been chosen by a single person and there was likely less oversight in the hiring process. This is not to say that visiting faculty members are not brilliant and quality teachers. It only means that the process they went through to be hired may not have been as rigorous.

The third category of faculty is adjunct or part time lecturers/professors. These professors only teach one or two courses per semester and may have other full time employment elsewhere. Colleges use part time professors because they are inexpensive (they are paid by the class), have expertise in a specific area that the full time faculty do not have, and/or because they can bring real world experience into the classroom. It is important to note that these are only categories of professors and how they are hired but do not describe how well those faculty members teach.

Given this information, what is the quality of the faculty at the school you are thinking about going to? For example, what is the percentage of faculty with a terminal degree (most often, a Ph.D.)? The average over the past twelve years is 72% (Carter, 2013). What is the percentage of faculty that are either tenured or tenure track both college-wide and in your potential major? What percentage of faculty both college-wide and in your potential major are adjunct or part time? What percentage of departmental courses are taught by a faculty member or graduate teaching assistant? While there are no real 'benchmarks' in relation to the quality of a faculty, you will want to look for a college and department with higher percentages of full time tenured or tenure-track professors and take these percentages into consideration. You will be able to get some of this information by examining web pages but information missing can be augmented by conversations with a faculty member once you visit.

Academic Support Systems

All colleges have departments whose primary goal is to support the academic program. These include academic skills centers and career centers, and even study abroad programs. You are going to want to see what kind of support you can get while you are in school. Academic skills centers (which go by a variety of names) can help with everything from writing and tutoring, offering quiet places for testing, dedicated assistance for those with learning disabilities and assistance with learning strategies. Career centers can help in securing internships and assist with resume building and job placement. A strong study abroad program gives you the opportunity to live and study in a different country for an entire semester. There is absolutely no comparison to visiting a country with family and actually living in a different country for four months. If you can afford to study abroad, including it in your college education is a must. If you have a country in mind that you would like to study in, it cannot hurt to ask your admissions counselor if the college has a program in that country.

Most, if not all, colleges will have each of these opportunities. The question you have to ask is how much or how many services do they offer. You can and should ask many questions. If you cannot find information on their website or do not make some phone calls during your research process, a good time to ask them is during your tour. The next chapter will discuss the campus visits.

Extra-Curricular Opportunities

This is an often-overlooked factor in choosing a college. Academics and (possibly) athletics may be more important but what other extra-curricular opportunities the college offers can be just as valuable. I hope that you will spend a great deal of time studying but even when you do, there will always be time left over for extra-curricular activities. These include intramural sports, student organizations and clubs, student government, and volunteer or service work. For the decision you are making now, a little research to see what opportunities the colleges offer can go a long way and should be considered when making your decision.

Tuition Versus Actual Cost of Attending

A discussion of choosing a college would not be complete without addressing the cost of attending college. Your choice might be ruled by the relative costs of tuition, books, and living expenses. This might mean living off campus or attending a state school whose tuition will likely be substantially less than tuition at a private school. This may mean going to a community college for two years and paying even less than a four-year state school and then attending a four-year institution to receive your bachelor's degree. This is a frank discussion that you should have with your parents whether you are paying yourself or your parents are paying all or some of your costs.

Remember, very few students pay the 'sticker price' at their college. According to an annual study conducted by the National Association of College and University Business Officers, 87.7% of freshmen obtained an institutional grant or aid in the 2012-2013 academic year and that number is slowly on the rise (Pullaro, 2015). Moreover, the average discount rate for incoming freshmen was 44.8% in the same year and that number too is slated to rise. This means that the college takes this percentage off the top of the full tuition price by giving out institutional grants, or merit aid. In short, you will not pay this amount. Whether your parents are paying or not, actual cost, any loans you will be taking, and institutional aid/scholarships you would be getting are very important considerations.

The Value Analysis

Outside of tuition, there is another financial factor you should take into account. Think hard about the relationship between the college you choose to go to and what job you will have after college. You will need to think this through because it should make a difference in your decision. Some professions necessitate a ranked undergraduate college and you may need to attend a specific school in order to excel in the field that you plan to enter. On the other hand, attending a highly ranked school may have less impact on your job or graduate school search. For example, if you want to be an elementary school teacher or biologist, it might not matter which undergraduate school you attend but if you want to be a politician, a ranked school will be important. If you want to be a law clerk for a U.S. Supreme Court Justice, you will likely have to attend a top ranked law school but if you want to be a criminal defense attorney, you will not need to attend a top tier school.

The reason this is important is the amount of money you choose to spend on your undergraduate education must be taken into consideration with your career path. For example, if you plan to become an engineer, you may want to consider a ranked (and possibly expensive) college since job placement in that specific field may be strongly dependent on your undergraduate education. Conversely, if you plan to become a middle or high school teacher, then attending a very expensive, ranked college may not be the best decision you can make. You may end up $30,000 - $60,000 or more in debt and only be making $40,000 - $50,000 per year. Your loan payment will quite likely be more than you can afford. If you plan to go to law school, it may less important which undergraduate college you go compared to what you do when you are there.

The fewer loans you have when you graduate, the more money you will have to spend on rent, mortgage, food, etc. Put it this way, as of July 2017, the total outstanding student loan debt (both federal and private) in the United States is over one and a half *quadrillion* dollars (FinAid, 2017). Work to add as little as you can to that number.

Lastly, keep in mind that it will be your degree, GPA, and possibly the college's ranking that will get you your first job. After your first job, those two factors will likely become less and less important. What jobs you have and your performance in those jobs will begin to take on a more important role than the college you attended.

Location

While location may not be your primary concern, it is a factor should be taken into account. By location, I am referring to both the college setting and the distance the college is from home. In regard to the setting, do you want an urban, rural, or suburban setting for your college? Colleges in urban areas have much more around them to be involved in, while with rural colleges, you may be relying on the extra-curricular activities, clubs and organizations that the college offers. Colleges in the suburbs or at the outskirts of cities may be able to offer both.

You should also think about how far you want to be from your current home. If you plan to live at home while attending school, then location becomes less relevant. If you are planning to go away to college, distance matters. In 2014, the majority of first year students attended college within 100 miles from home and this (57%) has not significantly changed over the last forty years (Eagan, Stolzenberg, Ramirez, Aragon, Suchard, and Hurtado, 2014).

Being close to home allows you the ability to be near family and familiar surroundings but also allows for over-reliance on family members. Even if you do choose a college very close to home, it will be important to limit home visits on weekends since it will take away from the important social aspect of college. The further you move away from home, the more reliant you will need to be on yourself and your new support structure. An important part of the college education experience is growing into adulthood and becoming independent, and location can play a part in the process.

Athletics

If you plan to be involved in NCAA athletics, you are not alone and for some, this may be the primary factor that you take into account when choosing a school. That being said, only approximately 6%-7% of high school athletes will go on to compete at the college level and only 2% of high school athletes will be awarded an athletics scholarship (NCAA, 2016). In fact, you may have already decided which college you plan to play for and if so, this may make many of the other categories listed here irrelevant. If you do plan to play a sport but have not chosen a college to play for, there are separate considerations to take into account. These may include the strength and record of the team, the college's recruitment efforts, and any scholarship offered, among others.

What is important to remember is that while you are playing for a team, you are going to be in college and will need to prioritize academics as well and it would be unwise to lose focus of that during your research. The tendency is to focus primarily on the sport and not on your studies and this could be very detrimental. Think about it this way, if you do not prioritize academics and fail out of college, you will not be playing for the team. While this will be addressed later in this book, suffice it to say that there is a high probability you will not go pro and given that, it is going to be crucial that you be a student who is also an athlete rather than an athlete who happens to be taking classes.

Make a List

After you have done your research and before you visit your first college, make a list of questions you are going to ask on your visit. At this point, you have likely read the websites (hopefully thoroughly) from colleges you are interested in. You have also thought about your priorities and narrowed the number of colleges you plan to visit to a manageable list. You are now at the point where you are ready to start thinking about college visits and tours. A significant benefit of narrowing down the number of colleges is that it significantly reduces the number of tours you go on. This is beneficial because after several, they get very repetitive and that may put the schools on the end of your tour schedule at a disadvantage. In other words, a school you may have been very interested in becomes less enticing to you because it is at the end of a long season of touring. The college visit tour can also get very expensive for you and your parents.

So now, it is time to make a list of questions. This list should be made up of questions that came to light when you were doing your research. These will likely include more general college life and academics questions and also questions that are specific to one particular college on your list. They need to focus around your priorities and what you feel is important in a college.

These questions should be pointed and clear. They should not be ones that you could have obtained answers for with a bit more research. They should be written down as to not be forgotten and answers to those questions should be written down as well. After several tours, colleges will start to blend in together so getting the answers down on paper during your visit is important.

If you have any significant questions where the answer might make you rethink your decision to have that school on your short list, you should call the relevant person at the college to get your question answered. These may include questions about tuition and the tuition discount rate, availability of scholarships, likelihood of making the team, or any other question that is important enough to ask *before* you make the trip to visit. If the answer is not what you wanted, expected or needed to hear, that school should come off your list. This would save you both time and money since it would eliminate the need to further research or visit that particular school. It would be a shame to drive or fly to your college visit only to ask your question and then realize that you do not want to attend there. This is a big decision and there are questions you should have answered prior to going on any college tour.

Lastly, there is one more thing to consider prior to visiting the colleges you are interested in. Do not visit your top choices first. This may sound strange. Think about it this way, with the first one or two colleges (usually the ones you are most interested in), you may not know what questions to ask simply because you have never taken a college tour before. So why would your first tours be the colleges you want to attend the most? In my opinion, it would be better to have those tours near or at the end of your college visits. The reason is that you want to know the right things to ask and the right things to look for on your tour and even with all the questions you've written down, there is nothing like going on several college visits to assist in making an educated decision.

I would suggest that your first visit be to the college that you want to go to the least. If your list is a very short list, then I would suggest going on a tour to a local college that you may not even apply to. This gives you the experience touring and at the very least, gives you a baseline to compare later colleges to.

On a side note, this is a great technique for job searching after you graduate. It is unlikely that you will have had a formal interview for a full time job in your field prior to graduation. To gain experience in job hunting and interviewing, apply for some jobs you don't want (that you may be overqualified for) and go through the interview process with them. Mock interviews are helpful but there is no substitute for the real thing. When I graduated from college, I applied to be a prison guard so I could go through the interview process and background check. While I was never going to be a prison guard, I wanted to see where my weak points were in the job application process. It helped. One year later, I got a job as a New York State Trooper, my dream job. This same concept holds true for college visits.

Conclusion

For whatever reason you have, some of you will know exactly where you want to go and know that you will be accepted. For most, however, you will not know what college you will be attending and will apply to several. The considerations above would be most beneficial if you think about them prior to applying to different schools. Not only will you save application fees and costs associated with visiting college campuses, but it may also help you to add colleges that were not on your original list and eliminate colleges from your list that don't fit your priorities.

Research is an important first step in making a choice of where you want to go to college and the research should certainly be done prior to any visits. It is easy to be swayed by the beauty of a campus or the friendliness of the tour guides or other campus representatives but you have to know about the school before you tour there. The research is not that hard, I promise. It will take you some time but the benefits will be substantial. I feel that once you start your research, it will get easier and easier and I hope you find my suggestions helpful.

Choosing a College –
The Campus Visits

Introduction

College visits can go one of two ways. The first way is for you to allow the college to guide your experience. You will sit down with an admissions and/or student finance counselor, complete a tour, perhaps eat lunch, and maybe even sit in on a class. You will get a good feel for the campus, but remember, each college is going to try to 'sell' you on themselves. As such, you will get all the good and none of the bad.

The second way is for you (not your parents) to guide your own experience. Go through all of the above but make choices to speak to people that are important to you. It is your visit and you have the chance to make the most of it. Since colleges are working to guide you toward choosing them, they will likely work as hard as they can to accommodate your requests that may be outside the 'normal' college tour they offer.

You want to see if the college is a good fit for you and if you are a good fit for the college. Sometimes, a campus will just 'feel right' to you and while that is a good start, there is still work to do. Finding out if a college is right for you moves beyond just touring the campus. Remember the old adage that you cannot judge a book by its cover? Well, that applies equally to colleges and college visits as it does to people you have just met. You have to dig deeper into the college and work to get an inside look on your visit. Once you do, you will be ready to make a strong, informed choice about the colleges you do want to attend and those that you do not.

The Visit

The first important piece of information you need for your visit is this: It is *your* college tour and not your parent's college tour. While you can gladly have them tag along, it is your education and you need to take the lead. Even if this is difficult for you, think about the college visit as a non-confrontational, relaxed place to start your movement toward independence. While there may be financial issues that parents will have to discuss with a student financial aid office, there is no other area where they should be taking the lead. This should all be about you.

When I was the director of my college's first year center, I was manning a sign-in table at an orientation for prospective students. A mother and son came up and though I directed questions to the son, the mother answered every question. I took the son's folder that the mother was carrying and handed it to the son and told him to take control of his own education starting now. I do not think the mother was very happy with me but that lesson needs to be learned.

The second important piece of information is this: College is a business and they each want your business. Put another way, colleges want you to apply and if accepted, they want you to attend. Smaller schools are tuition driven. This means that the bulk of their operating budget comes from what they make from tuition…and they want your tuition. You may ask yourself what this means for the college tour. It means that they are going to sell you on the college. They are going to tell you all the great things about the school, show you the things that make them stand out, and make you want to go there. If schools are contacting you repeatedly (by whatever method), this should make it clear. If not, the tour will.

There will probably be parking spots with your name on it, friendly staff in the admissions offices to greet you, and very friendly and outgoing students to give you the tour. There are different models that different colleges use but make no mistake; they want the tour to seal the deal for you. This is another reason that going on a tour of a college you *do not* want to attend can help you make your choice. You want to be experienced enough to see through the sales pitch and get to know the college in relation to your needs as it compares to other schools. *Your* priorities (from the first chapter) should be the key and should guide your actions and your questions. You certainly do not want to miss the tour of the campus but you also want to make the most of your visit by getting the information that is important to you. Move beyond what is shown to you through the windows. Go inside and learn as much as you can.

With that in mind, here are some pointers so you can maximize your visits to colleges.

The Importance of a College Map

You are going to want to download and print a map of the college or obtain one from the admissions office. While you are not going to get lost during you tour, the map holds a very important function. You will likely be living on campus and if so, there will be options for you to live in different residence halls. At most colleges, some halls are desired while others are less so. You will want to ask the tour guide, which residence halls students prefer while taking into consideration what buildings your classes are in and how close they are to your dorm. Where is the cafeteria, student center and workout facilities? Is there parking close by? The weather will not always be nice and there will likely be times when you are running late for class. Requesting a residence hall that is conveniently located is a choice you want to consider during your tours. You won't sign up for housing until later in the summer but if you can request a certain residence hall, isn't it smart to think ahead of time and make an informed choice that will make your life easier?

When to Visit

You will want to visit when school is in session and not on a Friday. You'll likely have read this online someplace else and it's great advice. You want to see the campus when at its busiest. You want the campus to be bustling with students and faculty and maintenance workers. This only happens during the regular academic year excluding holiday and summer breaks. Make sure to ask the admissions person prior to making your appointment because colleges have short breaks during the year and while the admissions staff will still be working, students and faculty will not be around.

The same holds true for the day of the week you visit. In college, the classes do not meet every day at the same time. You may have a class on Tuesday and Thursday at 1pm or on Wednesday night at 8pm., Colleges schedule courses in such a way as to maximize use of the number of classrooms they have so classes are spread out over the week during the day and evenings. At my school, I teach a three-hour class during the afternoon and then another that ends at 10:00pm. That being said, there will always be fewer classes scheduled at night and on Friday (who wants classes on a Friday anyway?) and as such, there will be fewer students and faculty around.

Listening and Asking Questions

Listen to everything that the students, faculty, or admissions counselors say. Listen intently because it can tell you a great deal more than just hearing. As I stated above, they are going to tell you the best things about the school and why you should attend. They will generally not say negative things about the school. Once you listen, ask as many questions as you can. Think about channeling the inner five-year old in you by asking *why* as much as you can. You will get much more in-depth answers if you do. You will force the tour guide or admissions counselor to explain and expand. You will get them to engage more in a conversation than a recorded speech and those answers should lead you to even more questions. In short, there is absolutely no substitute for asking about why some facet of the college is what they say it is. For example, your tour guide may indicate that there is a great sense of community at the school. Well, what makes it that way? Ask. The admissions counselor may say that their college has a great faculty. Ask why. Are they great and renowned scientists and scholars or great teachers? You will get so much more information by asking questions that engage others into a conversational answer. Please let this pointer guide you at all stages of your college visit.

The Tour

Go on the tour and ask questions. The tour should be the least important part of your visit. You should ask questions but remember that your tour guides will likely be handpicked students who are trained to show the college in the best light. Let them do their job. Just be sure to be respectful to the tour guide. They are not making much money walking backwards for an hour.

Eat in the Cafeteria

The food may or may not be gourmet but the food is not the reason you should eat there. You should have lunch in the cafeteria with current college students. Do this without your parents. They will be able to find a place to eat lunch but it is important that you have lunch in the student cafeteria without them. If you want honest answers from college students, having parents at the table may not be the best option. It may be difficult for you to approach a group of students and ask to eat with them but it is worth it. If it is too hard, find a person who is sitting alone and ask to sit with them. That might make it a bit easier and you can still ask all the needed questions.

Sit in on Classes

Ask to sit in on at least two classes with two different professors. If you do not have time for two, it is an absolute must to sit in on at least one class and you should have no campus visit without it. In order to get a representative idea of what classes are like, sitting in on one class may not be enough. For example, if you sit in on a class where the professor is active and fun, and where the students are awake and engaged, it may sway you toward that school. That is a great reason to go to that particular college but if that professor is the exception and not the norm, then you are not obtaining all the information you need to make a sound decision. The opposite is even truer. Not picking a college because you sat in on one dud of a class should not

41

happen. By sitting in on two classes and talking to active students about classes and professors, you will get a much stronger view of what academic life at that college is like.

The benefits of sitting in on classes are many.

➢ **You get to see what a class at that particular school is like.** Some will be large classes with lecture style and some will be small with a more involved body of students. The more classes you visit at different schools, the more you will get an idea of what type of class you could best learn in.

➢ **You get to see how professors and students interact with each other.** Are the classes more discussion-based? Have the students done their homework and are they participating in a meaningful fashion? Alternatively, is the professor just lecturing and not involving the students? Avoid thinking about the workload for a course or courses and instead focus on the teaching. You're going to work hard in college and you might as well attend one where you have strong, smart faculty that teach in a way that best suits your learning style.

➢ **Sitting in on classes in the major you intend to declare is twice as beneficial.** Not only do you get an idea of what classes are like, you get to see what classes in your major will be like. Additionally, you will meet the faculty members who teach those courses, and in college, you are more likely to make stronger connections with faculty from your major than faculty who teach in other majors. Making the connection now can help your transition once you arrive at the college for the fall semester.

I would strongly suggest planning your visit around your class visits. It would be most beneficial if you could find out when the introductory course to your intended major is being taught. Find this out yourself by navigating to the college's course schedule page rather than asking the admissions counselor. Then plan your visit so you can sit in on that particular class.

Talk to People

a. Talk to Students Outside Academic Buildings and Who Are Not Tour Guides

Some of the free time on your visit day will likely fall between classes or when no classes are scheduled. Students will be hanging around academic buildings talking. Approach them and ask them questions about the college. You do not have to be shy here. They will be happy to talk to you. You can ask about academics, sports, social life, or the residence halls but whatever you ask, make sure that the questions are based on your priorities from the last chapter. Just get them talking about the college and you will learn more than you can imagine.

By talking to several students, you'll get a much better understanding about the way students feel compared to speaking to just one other student or the tour guide. Some may love the school and others may not. The one thing you do not want to do is base your judgment of the school on the comments of a single student because it simply may not be representative of how the student body feels overall.

b. Talk to Students in your Prospective Major or Majors

You may have already decided on a major or you may even have two in mind. If that is the case, then it would be smart to speak with more than one student in each of those majors. The admissions office should be able to set that up for you and if not, you could likely find students who are majors in the class you sit in on. Ask about the courses, professors, and major you are thinking about. Remember; always speak to more than one student to get a more complete view.

c. Sit Down with Faculty Member(s)

This is incredibly important and I cannot stress it enough. Speak to one or two faculty members in the department you plan to major in. If you are not sure of what major you are going to declare, work to speak to a faculty member in a subject area that interests you. Since you have already sat in on a class or two in the department you think you will major in, it would be smart to sit down with the professor from that class. On a side note, if the college cannot make that happen, it should tell you something about the commitment to the students that a college's faculty have (or don't).

Please notice that I labeled this section as 'sit down with' rather than 'interview' a faculty member. This is a conscious decision because it should not be seen as an interview. The word 'interview' generally implies that one person is seeking a job or some consideration from the other person. In this case, while you are seeking information, it is in a much more informal setting and the pressure of an interview should not be on you. I am just suggesting that you have a very informal conversation about the major.

Many of the high school students that have requested to sit down with me are very nervous when they walk into my office. The tension is palpable and you can feel it. From my point of view, while I understand the nervousness, there is no need for it. We are just teachers at a different level than you are used to and have little no or no impact on acceptance decisions. This may differ at larger research institutions (where there are faculty researchers) but in smaller schools, we are just teachers who would be more than happy to sit down with you for a half hour. If the professor you sit down with clearly does not want to be there, that could indicate that you might not want to attend that college. This is another reason you should speak with two faculty members.

You will likely ask questions about the college, the major, and students but it is the point of having a conversation that is most important. At the very least, you learn more about the college from a faculty perspective rather than from an admission perspective. On a higher level, you have actually just made a personal connection with a professor who you may have several courses with and/or who may end up being your advisor. You will likely be able to contact that professor directly without needing to go through admissions (do not forget to get a card with their contact information on it and be sure to send a thank you email). You also can (and absolutely should) ask the professor if he or she can send you syllabi from a few courses, including the introductory course.

Along with sitting in on classes, this is the most important thing you can do during your college visit. Your college education will be guided by professors so

45

feeling good about them before walking in the door your first day is crucial for you. Visiting classes and speaking with faculty is the best way to get a solid perspective on the academics at the colleges you are thinking of attending.

Other Important Places to Visit

a. Student Center

Are there central areas where students can congregate? What amenities do they have in the student center? Comfortable seating areas? Student mailboxes? Food? Pool tables? If this is going to be the place where you will likely hang out, make sure it seems comfortable to you. Check outside the center as well. If it is warm out, make sure there are places outside the student center to relax in.

b. Study Abroad Office

Most study abroad semester programs cost the same tuition as you are already paying so it makes little sense *not* to go abroad during your four years as an undergraduate. Stop in and see where they have both faculty-led programs (one where a faculty member goes with a group of students) and outside agency led programs (where another school or study abroad provider leads the group). Both have their advantages and disadvantages and asking staff about study abroad opportunities now can help you make a decision.

c. Academic Skills Center

These centers are where any student can get help with college success skills (i.e. time management, study skills, etc.) and where students with learning disabilities get assistance and accommodations. Generally, these centers offer assistive technologies, professional tutors, study spaces, quiet testing spaces, computers, learning strategies courses or assistance, and time management strategies. It would be good to find out what services they offer because even if you do not have a learning disability, you will find their services beneficial.

d. Public Safety

You should ask for the most recent few years of the college's Clery Report. This is a federally mandated report focusing on how much crime exists on campus. When looking at the reports from several colleges, make sure you look at the proportion of crime (to the total student population) rather than the raw numbers. Also, looking at more than one year gives a more complete picture.

e. Student Financial Aid Office

You're likely already planning to meet with them but this is where you can talk about the tuition package they will offer, any merit scholarships (or other scholarships) that the school offers that you may be eligible for, and any special programs (i.e. honors programs) that allow for tuition discounts. Get as much information as you can and you may be able to save a significant amount of money.

f. Career Center

Since your plan is to have your education train and teach you about a profession you intend to go into, it's important to visit the college's career center to determine what assistance they can give you while you're in school *and* after you graduate. Ask about their job placement rate generally and in relation to the major you intend to declare. Ask about what services they offer (i.e. resume building, internships) while you're in school and it's just as important to ask about the services, if any, they can offer you *after* you graduate. Some college career centers offer assistance for life and that is important to know.

Conclusion

The college visit season can be a difficult one. A lot of travel may be involved in your college search. If you are looking in a specific region that is a bit away from your home, you may be taking a few days to a week and touring several colleges. This will get tiring and burdensome. Try not to let your tour exhaustion impact how you feel about the schools you are visiting. Work hard not to let one visit sway you completely toward that school because it was one of your first college visits. You may very well end up attending that school there but making an informed decision means taking your time and comparing schools. Once you are done with your visits, this will be your next task.

After you have finished your college tours, it is time to think about where you want to attend. After you have examined all of the factors that are important to you and have made college visits, begin to hone down the list of colleges you will apply to or have been accepted into. Prioritize the factors that are most important to you. Write these down and assess each of these priorities with the colleges of your choice. While pro versus con list or a matrix can help organize, write these out in whatever form suits you best.

Once you have done that and you narrowed it down to one or two schools, it would be a good idea to take another quick visit to your top school or schools. While you do not need another tour, questions may have surfaced that you did not think to ask during the first visit. This second visit gives you the opportunities to ask those questions. You should also sit in on one more class from a different professor and meet a different professor who teaches in the major you plan to declare. I know this sounds like a pain but it is advantageous given that the next four years of your life will be based on this single decision.

Yes, this process takes a great deal of time, energy, and at times, money and you may not complete the entire process before deciding on a school. While I know that going through the full process can lead to a solid, well-informed decision, I am a realist and practical professor and know my way may not be the best way for you! My only request is that you work hard enough to make the informed decision rather than deciding too quickly without all the relevant facts.

If you do attend a school that you end up having concerns with, it is not the end of the world. Transferring is an option that many students take. While we as faculty want you to stay at our college, if it is right for you to transfer, I will always support that move.

Differences Between High School and College

Introduction

I cannot count the number of students who have come through my door on the first day of college and tell me that they did great in high school so college will be a breeze. They are confident and tell me that college will not be a big deal. I hate to say it but they can be the students that seem to struggle the most.

You may think that college is simply an extension of high school and this is quite normal. You have been in the public or private school system for twelve years and have understood the norms, rituals, habits and rules that have existed. If you look back to your earlier school years, they have not changed all that much from year to year. So, when thinking about

51

academics in college, it's easy to make the mistake that it will be similar to all your education up to now because that's all you've known.

If this is what you are thinking, you could find yourself mistaken. While some high schools are better at preparing students for college than others, college is different from high school in more ways than it is similar. From academic expectations to social life, understanding these differences before you show up on day one will be crucial in helping ease the transitional issues that you will likely have. Just about every incoming college first year student will encounter problems related to the transition but not everyone will have the same problems. Some may sleep until two or be a bit too social, and others may dive in to work or athletics more than they should. While I will speak to the transition to college later, take note that college is drastically different from high school. For now, I will just say that learning to balance, while not taking the newly found freedom you have for granted, will be crucial. You are going to have to re-learn many things so thinking about it now can help.

This chapter will focus on these differences and will be divided into four distinct sections. The first section will outline the differences in relation to your academics and workload. The second section will focus on what professors expect from you compared to high school teachers. The third section will focus on other academic differences not related to workload or professors and the last section will address the new found freedom you will have as a college student.

Academics

You may have heard about English teacher David McCullough Jr. and his speech to the 2012 graduating class of Wellesley High School, the school he teaches at. His speech started much like every other graduation speech in a congratulatory tone. Then he said this: *"All of this is as it should be, because none of you is special. You are not special. You are not exceptional."* *(Brown, 2012)* *If you've not read it, it's short and worth the time (*http://theswellesleyreport.com/2012/06/wellesley-high-grads-told-youre-not-special/*)*. I say this because that concept runs through many of the differences outlined below. As faculty, we want you to be special but only you can make yourself special by showing up and doing the work that we ask of you. To receive an 'A' in college, you have to consistently work very hard. To get an 'F' in college, you have to work just as hard (by consistently not working). Grades are not determined by effort and instead are determined by product. So, no matter how hard you work or how many hours you put in studying or writing a paper, it is what you submit that we use to determine your grade. While some courses will be easier or have less work than others, your work ethic and ability to get work done will be required and the responsibility is solely on you. We will not chase you down or send you numerous reminders of work you have to submit. With the specifics of the assignment and the due date clear, we simply expect that you will complete your work.

Please do not take this to mean that we are not there to help. On the contrary, we love when students come to our office and ask questions or get clarification on something discussed in class or an assignment. It is refreshing to have a student come in and show us their lecture notes to make sure they are understandable before they start studying for the test.

By coming in to speak to us, you are showing that you care enough about your work to go the extra mile and faculty appreciate that.

Workload

There are two primary differences between high school and college in relation to the workload. First, the workload will be much more demanding; you will read more, write more, be expected to keep track of your own work and be expected to have read and understood the material, even if we do not speak about it in class. We expect that you know that everything is testable and that many of us do not give review sheets. You may have fifty to one hundred pages (or more) to read between classes. You will have 10 to 15 to even 20+ page papers. It will be the norm not the exception.

a. Reading

You will be doing a great deal of reading in college. Reading takes time and you have to make the time for it. You will buy the textbooks and they will be expensive. Some of you will try to share textbooks to save money but that might not work out for you come test time. The reading might also be complicated and difficult to understand and depending on your major, may be scientific in nature. The natural sciences (i.e. biology) will certainly be technical and require a great deal of memorization. The social sciences (i.e. sociology, psychology) will require you to read mathematically based research. With both, they are difficult but learnable. While in high school, you read textbooks written for high school students, that is not always the case in college. You will read college textbooks but many of us use fiction or non-fiction books, academic journal articles, and other sources where you will have to pull the information out of the reading rather than have it given to you. You may be asked to watch movies or videos and be expected to analyze them in context with the specific class. You will have to acclimate yourself and be prepared to have homework that is for lack of a better word, non-traditional.

We expect that you do all the reading every time and know that you will be held responsible for all of it, even if we do not discuss it in class. Most professors do not have the time in one semester to address all the information and reading that we want to so we err on the side of giving you more reading to do than giving you less. If we do not get to lecture or discuss it in class, we still think it is important because we assigned it. Just as an FYI, if you do not come prepared to class because you haven't bought the book yet, your professor will likely have little sympathy (so borrow a book or ask a classmate if you can scan the readings ahead of time).

b. Quizzes

Professors expect you to read and if you do not, your grade can be impacted in a significant manner through quizzes. Some of us give quizzes and some do not. Many professors will give quizzes regularly and some professors may or may not announce their quizzes. We need you to come in prepared and quizzing allows you to demonstrate that to us. Some will give handwritten quizzes and other will give electronic ones. In most of my classes, I give short, timed electronic quizzes on a learning management system or LMS[1] before each class period when a new reading is due. Rather than give unannounced quizzes, I force you to read before you come to class because a significant portion of your grade is based on those pre-class quizzes. From a faculty perspective, this has changed my life as a teacher. It is awesome for me! Instead of speaking to a room where 50% or less have read, just about every student reads the assignment before class. This increases participation and leads to much more in-depth discussions that benefit everyone. In many classes, quizzes can significantly hurt your grade if you choose not to read the assignments for the day.

c. Examinations

As I stated above, you will be tested on everything that was assigned, regardless of whether you discussed it in class. Different professors prefer different exam types so you will have to navigate tests that are short answer, multiple choice, true/false, short essay, and long essay (note: If a professor gives you the option between multiple choice tests or essay/short essay tests, always choose the essays. We can give partial credit on essay exams but not on multiple choice. We are also excellent at making very difficult multiple-choice questions. Just keep that in mind). Tests can be in class, take home, or take home long papers. In some of my upper level courses, exams are 10 page take home papers with only one or two

---

[1] A LMS is a web based application to deliver educational material. Think about how you might access class materials if you were to take a 100% online course and you've got the idea of a LMS. Most schools have them and most professors use them.

questions. Remember, a good portion of your grade will likely be determined by examinations.

You will be better at some types of examinations than others and while you won't be able to cherry pick all the classes you're going to take according to the exam type, you may be able to ease your pain by researching how a professor tests before signing up for the class. At many colleges, past syllabi are posted online and if not, you can always email the professor directly and they will likely get back to you.

In my lower level courses, I actually deduct points for spelling errors on in class exams (and yes, I let them use a dictionary). Based on my end-of-semester student evaluations, it is very clear that students generally are not big fans of this but I tell them that you cannot always rely on your word processor when you are out of college. If you are not a good speller, then I am suggesting that you work on it because if you start misspelling words on reports for your post-college job, you may find yourself jammed up. Why not start working at it now rather than relying on spellcheck (which will get you in trouble if you *only* rely on it).

d. Writing

This deserves repeating: It is incredibly important to become a good writer and in college, you should improve regardless of the level you write at in high school because you will write many papers. Writing is a skill that will follow you in every job and may well be one of the keys to success in college. From a professor's viewpoint, an "A" is both excellent in writing and content. A "B" is above average in both or excellent in one area and average in another. A "C" is average in both writing and content. If we cannot understand what you are trying to say because you struggle in your writing, we will not be able to grasp the information you are trying to convey. As such, you may not get the grades you want on written assignments and again, this will be regardless of the amount of effort you put into the paper.

In college, it is likely you will get the chance to turn in drafts of your work prior to submitting the final product. Some courses, English courses especially, will require drafts but in other courses, you will have opportunities to submit drafts. Most students do not submit drafts unless required but you absolutely should. Additionally, you should know that in many courses, your written assignments could make up the bulk of your grade. This is especially true in upper level courses where testing focuses on take home essays or big papers. With this in mind, why not work early and submit drafts? Your grade can only go up if you fix what we ask you to fix on your draft.

Lastly and as noted above, it is unlikely that we will hold your hand through the writing process. We make ourselves available but you have to be the one to take the initiative. In college, you will also be assigned term papers in the syllabus and that is the last you may hear of it until it's due. College professors expect that you can manage your time and assignments and that you do not need constant prodding or reminding. It is up to you to keep track of your work in all your courses but you can do it.

Professor Expectations in Class

a. Grades

In college, different professors have their own systems to calculate your grade and it will be up to you to understand it from the first day of the class. The key part of that sentence is the word 'calculate.' We do not make grades up in mid-air or let our feelings guide what your grade will be. We let the numbers do the talking. Just make sure you ask about the grading scheme if you have any questions.

b. The Syllabus

The syllabus in each of your courses is a contract. It tells you exactly what is going to be expected of you while at the same time telling you what you can expect from the professor. Once we hand it to you, we assume you have read and understand it. If you have a concern, the syllabus is what both you and the professor will rely on to help settle it. The problem is that every professor forms their syllabus differently than others and all have their own rules, including attendance and grading policies. One of my sophomore students told me that she really benefitted from bringing the syllabus with her to each class because she always knew what was going on and could always refer to it in class when she needed to.

c. Workload

The workload in some courses may be light but as you move from your first year to your senior year, the workload will be heavy, regular, and complex. Most professors will not give extra credit or extra time to hand in late work without penalty. Others will not accept any late work. You will absolutely have to earn your grade keeping in mind that a "C" is average. On another note less related to grades, it would not be a smart idea to rely on what other students say about a certain class or professor. They may have a completely different learning or test taking style and what works for them might not work for you. Approaching the professor and asking to see a past syllabus is a good idea when attempting to figure out what they expect from you (both in class and out).

d. In Class Behavior

We expect that you will conduct yourself like adults in the classroom. We do realize that you are only one very small step removed from high school but part of the college experience is you learning to act like an adult and that includes accountability. This means that making excuses for why you were on your phone, were disruptive in class, or did not submit work is going to be extremely problematic. As such, if the professor believes that you acted disrespectfully (even if you did not feel you were disrespectful), you will likely hear about it in a face-to-face setting. We find texting in class to be extremely disrespectful and in some classes; the penalties for getting caught texting or being on your phone will be severe. Personally, I take points away from your final grade if I catch you on your phone. There have been a few times where I have answered a student's phone in class and once, it was his mother on the phone. She was a bit shocked when I told her he was in class and could not talk right now. I think she had some choice words with him after class!

We also expect that you are mature enough to be able to support whatever your position a on an issue is with information from an academic source. Saying that something is true because you believe it to be true is not enough in college. Moreover, we expect that you can debate and discuss without taking it personally and without personally attacking another student whose views differ from yours. College is about learning about other peoples' points of view and we only ask that you are open to those ideas, regardless of whether you agree with them. Other than the hard sciences like biology, many of your classes will have these hard discussions and we want you to be able to think alternate ideas through.

Other Academic Differences

a. Class Schedule

In high school, you will spend seven or more hours going to and from classes, meals, athletics, and after-school activities. A college course schedule will be very foreign to you and will take getting used to because the times and days of your classes will change every semester. It is difficult but you should work on adapting to this new schedule every semester as fast as you can. As you get some semesters under your belt, you will be in a better place to figure out a weekly class schedule that works for you. One of my sophomore advisees told me that he hated it but had to accept that the schedules will change every semester.

First, your schedule will be staggered. By this, I mean that you will have classes at different times of the day and the schedule will vary all week. You may have three classes on one day and no classes the next. You may start at 8:30am on Monday morning but not until 2:30pm on Tuesday. You may have class until 10pm one day and then at 8:30am on the next. It is very unnerving when you first experience it because it is so much less regimented than the school schedule you have had for twelve years!

This type of schedule can be very difficult for new students because it equates to a great deal of free time when you do not have classes. It takes discipline to be comfortable in this type of schedule and to work during your free times. You will be tempted to sleep right up until class and to nap between classes. Avoid this at all cost until you know it will not negatively impact your studying time and classes.

In high school, your subjects and class times are generally set for you but in college, you will always have subject and schedule choices. In your first semester at college, however, you may end up with a schedule that is not ideal (i.e. early classes, few exciting course choices). This is because the returning students will have already registered. Once you are one of those returning students, your schedules will become more to your liking because you choose how to organize your days/evenings of class schedule (and studying time). Later in the book, I will describe how to get into classes that are already full. As a final note, you cannot always have Friday off. Sorry about that!

b. Time Commitment

College courses require that you will work a certain number of hours outside class – normally between 3-4 hours per hour of in class time. Some weeks it will be less and some it will be more but make no mistake, most of the learning in college comes outside of class. As noted above, if you choose not to study outside of class your grades will definitely suffer. It will take you a full year of college to begin to figure out a work/class/study schedule that works for you. Since you will not be in class seven hours a day as in high school, you will need to figure out what is most beneficial for you.

When I was in college, I worked to get all my classes scheduled at the same time five days a week (so I could get up at the same time every day) and I chose to study in my room with the radio on light static (to drown out any outside noises – I get strange looks every time I tell someone about that technique!). Keep in mind that it could be very frustrating but just be patient and know you will figure out a weekly class and homework schedule that works for you.

c. Professors are not Trained Teachers

College has a dirty little secret. Unlike every one of all your past and current teachers, college professors are not trained as teachers (unless they teach education studies). We are chosen because of the expertise we have in our discipline. This means that some college professors are brilliant but not very good at teaching. It is likely that when you declare a major and have to take several classes within that department, you are going to get some professors whose teaching style you love and some you do not. You win some and you lose some! At smaller institutions, teaching may be the primary focus of professors and many will be good teachers. At larger institutions, research may be the focus and while you may not get good teachers, you will get brilliant academics. As a side note, larger research universities may have professors that teach only one course a semester and while that professor's name is on the schedule, a graduate teaching assistant may be the one who is actually teaching the course.

I am not implying that colleges are full of terrible teachers. I am just saying that you will encounter professors whose teaching style is not the best for you and professors who are very smart but may not be the best at getting their points across (think about a very brilliant person who may not be the best at navigating social situations). Perhaps asking how professors are evaluated would be a smart question for a tour (or faculty interview) to see how much of their assessment focuses on their teaching.

d. Professor Availability

In high school, your teachers are generally available during school hours when they are not teaching. In college, professors do not work 9am-5pm (because, like yours, our schedules vary) and we are not always in their office when they are not teaching. In general, we must have a certain number of 'office hours' each week when we need to be in our office solely for the purpose of meeting with and helping students. At my college, we have to hold office hours for only five hours per week. This means that you need to know when those office hours are so you can come see us then. If you make an appointment with a college professor, it is important to show up prepared and on time. We find it very disrespectful if you choose not to show up when we have set aside time for you. You may get a sternly worded email (you would definitely get one from me) and if so, a face-to-face apology will be in order.

Make no mistake, during the academic semesters, professors put in many hours of work. We have to teach and grade but we also are on college committees and have other administrative duties wholly outside of teaching. We work hard but just may not do it in the office with the door open due to distractions. For example, I never teach on Thursdays and Fridays (my schedule works out this way) but I work at least 5-6 hours Thursday-Sunday at home. Do not assume we are not working when we are not in the office because the truth is that we will *always* have more homework than you starting on day one of every semester. You may have three papers to write and we will have 50 to grade. You want a test back immediately but it takes hours for us to grade the tests for the entire class. Please keep in mind that a professor might not respond to your communication immediately and work to be ok with that and know that we are doing the best that we can for you. Lastly, it is also less likely that we will read a draft of your paper right before its due (I require that all drafts be in two full weeks from the final due date. This gives me time to comment on it and get it back to you so you can make revisions). Did I mention how important it is to submit drafts?

e. Relationships with Professors

In high school, many of your teachers have Master's degrees but in college, most of your professors will have a Ph.D. in their field. This means that they have achieved the absolute highest degree in their field and it is a significant accomplishment. A

Ph.D. normally takes between five to seven years to complete and requires a very lengthy dissertation (generally 200-400 pages) that is original work in that person's field. To put the difficulty of a Ph.D. into context, in 2014, only 1.55% of all Americans over the age of eighteen have Ph.D.'s (U.S. Census Bureau, 2015).

This information is important because it may impact how a professor chooses to interact with you and how they expect you to behave. They may be very open and fun (this is how I am in and out of class) or they may be serious and aloof. Some may be more formal than others may. In any case, behaving in a respectful manner is vital. It is a rule you should not forget, even if you are upset with a professor for a grade or something they said in class.

Here are a few general rules to follow when dealing with college professors that may differ from what you are used to in high school. First, if a professor has a Ph.D., you should call them doctor or professor. If they do not have a Ph.D., you should call them professor. Even with professors who are less formal (i.e. allow you to call them by their first name); being polite and maintaining respect and decorum when communicating *in any form* with them is paramount. Second, you should never call a professor by only their last name and you should *never* write emails in text-speak. Also, you must proofread and spellcheck all your emails to faculty. Professional communication is expected of you in the working world so we expect you to do it in the collegiate world as well. Third, some professors will give you their home or cell phone numbers because they want to be available to you when they are not on campus (I do this). Never take advantage of this. Do not text (unless professor indicates that texting is acceptable), and do not call after 8:00pm (unless the professor indicates a time deadline). We are people too and have lives outside of the college.

If there is one thing out of this book that you should remember about college and life, this is it. Respect will breed respect. Disrespect will not. As an example, if a student is disrespectful to me (and it has happened), I send them an email which tells them to come to my office so we can discuss the "manner in which they choose to communicate with faculty." If you receive this email from me, I can guarantee that this will not be a very comfortable conversation for you but it is easily avoidable – just be respectful. That really does not happen that often. I think I have only done that a handful of times over twenty years of teaching.

One time when I was taking my freshman seminar class camping for the weekend, we stopped at my home to pick up some firewood. After meeting my wife, one of the male students told me that 'she was hot' (which she is). I told him "you never get to say that to me." He was not trying to be disrespectful but it still was! I will speak more to professional communications in Chapter 7.

f. Diversity of Viewpoint

In high school, you learn a great deal of information that is black and white, and memorization will be an important part of your learning. While you will get some of that in college, much of the information will move well beyond rote memorization. As you move into your junior and senior year, you will be asked to know the information, apply and analyze it beyond what you memorized. Unlike many high school classes, your answers in class must be in-depth and you will be expected to justify your point of view with much more than personal experience. As I have said before, you need to be open to the points of view of others even if you fully disagree with them. You never have to agree but we expect you show respect to your fellow students even when you may disagree with what they are saying.

Let me end this section with this note. There might come a time where you feel the professor disrespected you because, like you, we are human. In those instances, it is going to be important that you think about what was said and be sure that the comment was personal and not academic. If the professor expressed an academic viewpoint that you did not like, then that is not disrespect. If it was personal and you felt disrespected, that is different. My advice is to speak to the professor after class in private and express yourself in a cool and calm manner. We will listen, I promise.

Non-Academic Differences: Freedom

a. Freedom

Many of you are probably extremely excited about the freedom that college will give you, perhaps freedom that you do not have at home. You will have much more freedom than you have now and *you will make decisions* with little to no input from your parents. If you are living in the residence halls, your parents are not there with you and you will have many opportunities to do many things. There will be incentives not to do your homework and your parents will not be there to double check that you are finishing your work every night. In residence halls, friends will come to your room to socialize and there will be loud music somewhere that distracts you. You will also have more opportunities to sleep very late on days when you do not have classes and no one will tell you when to be home or go to bed. If you take advantage of all these different temptations, your academics will suffer. For now, keep in mind that you absolutely must balance your social and academic lives and you must understand that actions have consequences. Fail to keep these in mind and you may have an involuntary and unexpected exit from your college.

To be honest, if your parents have worked their tails off and are paying $5,000-$60,000 a year to put you through college, that is utterly disrespectful toward them. If you were paying for college yourself, then you would just be throwing money away. Put another way, if the tuition and fees were coming out of your pocket to the tune of $60,000, you would probably be working to do better in college. I will speak to this in much more detail in chapters 6 and 7 by giving you techniques to help balance your time and energies.

Conclusion

The purpose of this chapter was to show that there are clear differences between high school and college. Understanding them will help your transition to college life. This transition is problematic for so many college first year students and I have seen it demonstrated in several ways. Whether it be sleeping too much or too little, over-using alcohol or drugs, putting academics second, or emotional fallout from the transition, it is more difficult than you think it is. If you feel you will not be impacted by the transition, you are wrong. I am not saying that every college first year will struggle to the point of dropping out but I am saying that it is likely that transition issues will negatively impact you in some way.

I am not trying to freak you out but it's better to be prepared for the change rather than going in with mistaken expectations. I want you to succeed, pointing out these differences between high school and college can help de-mystify college, and your transition might be easier for you. In chapter 5, I will give you techniques that you can use to help ease the transition from high school to college. Heading to college with a stronger understanding of these differences can only help you.

Orientations

Introduction

Congratulations! You have decided on a college and have been accepted! You committed and paid a deposit to the particular school you plan on attending. Enjoy the summer and if you didn't already know, this summer will be your shortest. You will have much longer summers when you are in college. After most of the summer has passed, you will be headed to school, and preparing to go may be daunting for many. Remember, visiting the college is not the same as attending orientation or being a full time college student. You can do it! Remember it is a lot different from what you are used to.

During orientation, the focus moves away from the college trying to sell itself to you, and more toward the social, academic and administrative details of being a college student. There are aspects of college success that deserve attention here since all colleges hold some type of orientation sessions. In these orientations, colleges work to help prepare the incoming student before classes begin. They want you to be more familiar with what college is about and have you complete some of the administrative business before classes begin in the fall. They cannot prepare you for everything (and hopefully this book fills in the gaps) but they do try to lessen the impact of the transition as best they can.

Most colleges also bring in the new first year class a few days to a few weeks before the returning students come back to school. In these days before classes actually start, the focus shifts from educating you about what college life is like, to acclimating you to becoming a college student. So, the early orientations fulfill administrative functions and serve to introduce you to what college life is like along with having your first experiences with other incoming first year students. This chapter will focus on the spring and summer orientation opportunities that serve as your introduction to college life.

A Note About Parental Involvement at Orientation

Whenever I have a friend who tells me they are getting married, I always have the same advice about their wedding day. I tell them that it is their wedding day and not anyone else's day. While parents, in-laws, and friends want their voices heard, I tell them that they should be in control of how it goes. The same holds true for orientation and to be honest, college as a whole.

When you come to complete college tours, go to college orientations, or attend college, the operative word is not 'college' but instead, 'you.' It is *your* college education, acclimation, and knowledge. It is *your* experiences. It is *your* time and energy. You should be the one that is running the show, especially at orientation. (Are you starting to see a main theme of the book yet? Because this is it!). Think of it this way: This is your chance to demonstrate your individualism and independence, and by doing so, your parents may be less nervous about you leaving home.

In college circles, millennials have a reputation for being privileged and expect that they will do well in college because of their experiences in school to this point. This may not be your individual experience but we as faculty have seen some change toward this over the past few decades. Unfortunately, college is not like this. You will have to work and your parents will not be there to take control. So start now. Be in control at orientation, even though it may be a daunting experience. What better way to help yourself than to begin to overcome that nervousness now. Make it *your* education and if you have not already, begin during your orientations.

The question that you may be asking yourself is how to speak to your parents about this. My answer is to just have the conversation and be honest. As to when you should tell them, I would suggest well before you go to orientation so they are prepared and not taken by surprise. It is also beneficial because you and your parents can also have conversations about the orientation and things to look for and questions to ask. Asking their advice cannot hurt at all but just make it clear that you want to run the show at orientation.

Spring and/or Summer Orientations

College orientations come in many forms and at several times prior to the start of the academic year. Some schools mandate attendance and others make it optional. What you need to know first and foremost is *not* to miss one. For the reasons listed below, you will find that it is crucial that you attend. If traveling a good distance, it is still worth the trip if you have committed to a particular college or university.

Schedule Your Fall Courses

Most importantly, you will likely have the opportunity to schedule your courses for fall semester at your spring or summer orientation. Because all of the other current students have already registered, your selections may be quite limited. You rarely get the good ones when picking last. You may not get the classes that you want or the times when you want them. It is highly likely you will have to take an early morning class – sorry to be the one to tell you.

With this in mind, the earlier you can register for your fall courses, the better selection of courses you will get. You want to register before other incoming first year students because you are all fighting for the same limited number of open courses. So, the key will be for you to determine when the first orientation day will be and make sure you attend that orientation so you can register. Your first semester may depend on it. I cannot guarantee that you will get the ideal schedule with the ideal courses but I can say that you will be more likely to get better classes at better times if you do attend the earliest orientation.

Now, if you are concerned because you do not know what to take and how to register, don't worry, the college knows. Either the college will register you based on a list of course offerings and your interests or you will complete registration with help during the orientation. You will have the help of either a staff member in the college's first year department or a faculty member. They will help guide and advise you on your fall schedule. Just make sure that you get the name, phone number, and email of the college employee who helps you register so you can contact them directly if there are changes that need to be made. I would advise that you send a thank you email to keep you in their radar if you should need their further assistance.

a. Courses You'll Take in Your First Semester

In your first semester of college, you will likely have to take a first year seminar because colleges have some form of required common freshman course. While I will speak more to this in the next chapter, the good ones fill up fast, making early registration even more important. A colleague of mine teaches a CSI-based first year seminar and you can bet that fills up almost immediately.

You will also take two or three courses that go either toward your major or toward your general education requirements (i.e. math, science, humanities). If you know what your major will be, I suggest taking the introductory course to that major and one or two general education requirements. If you do not know what your major will be, take courses that fulfill those general education requirements but that also are in majors that you think you may want to declare later on. What you are doing is really testing the waters. You are seeing if a specific major interests you but if it does not, the class still fulfills a college requirement.

Finally, you will also have to take an English or composition course. There may be different levels and the one you will be placed in will likely be the result of your scores on your college's placement test or the SAT or ACT. Since there will be many sections (everyone has to take English), you will want to think about scheduling this particular course *after* you have chosen all other courses. That way you can fill out the times/days of your schedule in a manner that most suits you.

As I noted above, the other courses you will be signing up for may not be as desirable as you want given that all of the current students have already signed up. Even if the college's first year department reserves seats for incoming first years, it may not be that many spaces.

b. How to Get into Closed Classes

Here is a hint that may help you get you into the courses that you want, that are at the times you want to have them. This technique will work before you even get to college and will work every semester you are in school.

You will want to understand that the days and times of classes are spread out through the week in a very different manner than in high school. Classes that meet five days a week at the same time are extremely rare. Instead, they will be held two or three days a week. There may be separate science or language labs at a wholly different time as well. While you will need to get used to this manner of scheduling classes (which will be different for you every single semester), my advice here is geared toward classes and class schedule pages.

You must also understand how the class schedule web pages of your school are structured. There are different ways that they are set up but most have the same content. There will be information on the class itself (the class, department, name, number, day, time and professor somewhere on the page). More importantly here, there will be information on the course's enrollment. Basically, this refers to how many students are currently registered and the maximum number of students that can register.

These are the numbers you really want to pay attention to. If it is full or close to full, then you may not be able to get in during your orientation registration session. That being said, students definitely drop and add throughout the summer, so if the course is full at the time of your registration, keep going back to that class schedule page and see if anyone has dropped. If it were I, I would go back daily or every other day. Bookmark the web page. The thirty seconds it takes each day to look will be worth you getting into classes that you want. You do not want to take a class that you are forced to take because everything else is full.

If you go back to those web pages and see a spot open up, you can call or send an email to the college employee who helped you register (hopefully you saved their contact information) for your classes. If you did not, call the college's first year center. They can help as well. Respectfully ask if you can be moved into that open spot. It may not always work for you, but it cannot hurt to try. In the simplest terms, you want your first semester to be as good as it can be, so why not do a little work on the front end to make it happen.

c. Take an Extra One or Two Credit Class

You will want to consider taking an extra one or two credit class each semester, starting with your first semester at college. In most colleges, physical education, personal enrichment and college success classes are one or two credits and they are worth taking every semester. You will gain valuable credits toward graduation and if you do this every semester, you might be able to graduate a semester early (you would also need some thoughtful advising to make this happen). Many college students do not get enough physical activity and by taking a class that meets once or twice a week, you get exercise and that helps all around. College success skills classes are classes that everyone can benefit from. I've noted before, this is your first shot at college but faculty have been doing advising for years and can help guide you based on their experience.

I understand that it may not be right for you to take on that extra one credit course and that is fine. You may be a fall athlete and if so, you will have much less time due to workouts, practice and games. Others around (i.e. parents) may be worried that you would be taking on too much with the extra one credit class. Lastly, you may just want to go into your first semester with what the college considers a regular course load and that is ok. So, while I do recommend taking on an extra one or two credit class each semester (you will be happy in your senior year, trust me), your first semester may not be the right time.

d. The Times of Your Fall Courses

One other related topic must be addressed here. It is highly likely that you will have to take early morning classes. For the reasons listed above, your choices are going to be limited and the early morning classes generally have space in them because juniors and seniors avoid early morning classes like the plague! You may get lucky but do not count on it. The advice I will give is something that you should absolutely avoid doing. On the days you *do not* have morning classes, try not to schedule your first classes in the afternoon. This only promotes irregular sleep patterns and afternoon classes allow you to sleep a good portion of the morning away, a time when you could be getting work done. It is very difficult to get work done at night when socializing becomes more luring. Think about trying to get up at the same time each day and schedule your classes to facilitate this.

Take Placement Tests

The majority of colleges require you to take a course or two in math, languages, science, humanities, etc. These are called general education requirements and you will need to fulfill the different categories of requirements before you can graduate. In most schools, you will take your major, minor and these general education requirements (the requirements vary among different colleges but are very similar). The function of these classes is to have you graduate college with a well-rounded education. Being an expert in your major field is wonderful, but colleges want you to have general knowledge in areas that will help you in life.

Orientation is when you will likely have the opportunity to take placement tests. The placement tests seek to determine if you are proficient in a particular area (primarily math and language). If you can pass these tests, you will not have to take a class in that subject area. Passing the test will satisfy the requirement and getting any requirements out of the way before any college courses begin is a very smart move (AP and IB courses also can count toward college credits). Even if you are worried about getting a good enough score to place out, why not take it? You have everything to gain and absolutely nothing to lose other than an hour of your life.

Identification Cards and Technology Training

Your first few weeks of college will be stressful and full of experiences that are brand new to you. In short, do anything that you can to make yourself more comfortable when you arrive in the fall. You will see this advice later in this and other chapters as well. Having the opportunity to learn how to use the college's network and email system before you arrive in fall, will reduce the stress you feel in those first few weeks.

Financial Aid and Scholarships

Understanding how your college's financial aid system works and how much aid you are getting is important to know. While this may not be on the top of your list, it may be on the top of your parents' list. If the orientation does not include a meeting on financial aid, make sure you call ahead and schedule a session with a financial aid counselor. If it is your money, you will want to spend as little of it as you can and if it is your parent's money, they will feel the same way.

The other benefit of meeting with a financial aid counselor is that they will have information on college-specific scholarship opportunities. While there are hundreds of national level scholarships that you can apply for, all colleges have their own version of need and merit scholarships. You can apply for the scholarships that you qualify for. Get information on as many of these as you can, even those scholarships that may be only a few hundred dollars. Think about it this way, if it takes you three hours to complete an application for a scholarship worth three hundred dollars and you get it, you essentially just earned $100 an hour for your work (which translates to approximately a $200,000 annual salary). Not a bad trade off.

Lastly, make sure you obtain the financial aid counselor's name and contact information so you can send a thank you email after you get home. While you may say to yourself that they were just doing their job (and you would be correct), I want you to think about it looking forward. Financial aid workers hold the key to the money you are going to get (and everyone wants more money off their college tuition bill). Because of this, these workers have many negative encounters with students and parents. My advice is to get to know your financial aid counselor by name and stop by to do nothing more than to say hello every now and then. I am not saying it is going to get you more money but you are more likely to get a smiling face and better personal service if you go the extra mile.

Work Study Opportunities

Colleges have work study jobs. These are administrative jobs on campus that you can apply for. The federal government contributes toward what colleges pay student workers so there are always jobs on campus for students. The problem is that by the time the fall semester begins; most of the jobs have been taken. Like registering in summer, the benefit of searching for a work-study job early is that you beat all the other incoming first year students to the punch. Contact your school's student financial aid office in May or June if possible (you will be glad that you now have a friendly contact in the office). They will be able to give you the information work-study positions or forward you to the department that can.

If you obtain a work-study job, you will have money in your pocket and a job for your entire college career and I would suggest attempting to get a work-study position in the academic department you intend to major in if they are hiring. By doing this, you will get a better feel for the department and have a relationship with the professors outside of class. I always seek to hire incoming first year students for departmental work study positions because I would rather have someone reliable for four years than have to train someone every year. Moreover, I also only hire students who plan to major in criminal justice (my department). The key is to find the person responsible for hiring student departmental assistants and contact them directly (get the information from the financial aid office). If you can do this even prior to attending orientations, you have a better chance of getting the job because you will beat all the other incoming first year students who may have the same idea as you.

Majors and Student Organizations

During orientation, there will be an open house or two that give you the opportunity to research the different majors, college services and student organizations (i.e. academics, sports, Greek life, political, and social justice related) that are present on campus. Like many orientation activities, this allows you to make campus connections early. You will get to meet professors, help narrow down a potential major, and possibly join a student organization or two while you are there. Doing this helps ease stress once you arrive in August by giving you friends, professors you know, and more importantly, a support group of individuals who are already at the college you are going to attend.

Bring Vaccination Forms

Bring any forms or documentation the college requires you to bring. Vaccination records are usually the primary request. The college should send a request for any information but if they do not, those items should be listed on the college's website. If you still cannot find information on what you need to bring, call the coordinator of the college's freshman program – you will definitely find that on the college's website.

Sit in on a Class

If you have not already done so, you will likely have a chance to sit in on a class. This is more likely to happen during a spring orientation compared to a summer orientation. Even if you have observed a class during your initial visit, it is smart to visit another class, hopefully in your potential major. It is even better to sit in on a class with a professor that you have not seen teach before. Some colleges even hold shortened classes that both incoming students and parents can sit in on.

Stay Overnight in a Residence Hall

If there is an option to stay overnight in the residence halls, you should take it rather than spending the night in a hotel with your parents. Getting to know college becomes easier if you have spent a night among other students. If you are attending a spring orientation and school is in session, you will be placed with a current student and who better to give you an unedited and unscripted characterization of the school than a current student. This is your chance to ask questions and to learn what current students think about the college. Take note, however, you are only getting one viewpoint and as you will understand once you are in classes, one viewpoint may not necessarily be accurate. So, take the viewpoint in with caution and speak to other students to get a much deeper picture.

If you are attending a summer orientation when school is not in its full academic year, you will likely be placed with another incoming first year. This can be somewhat nerve wracking since you are both in the same uneasy position of staying overnight in a new place with someone you have likely not met before. It is worth it if only because you are both in the same position. You may not become the absolute best of friends (you never know) but you will get to know at least one person who you can reconnect with once you return and that is extremely important.

Regardless of whether you stay overnight at a spring or summer orientation, you will benefit. Go out of your comfort zone and be the person who sits at a cafeteria table with someone they do not know. Get involved in the icebreaker sessions you will inevitably go to. The benefits can be immeasurable.

The more you talk to other students, the more information you will learn and you will begin to gain a group of friends. The more you learn and gain a group of friends, the more comfortable you will be once you arrive in August. The more comfortable you are upon arriving, the easier the transition will be and an easier transition is something to strive for.

Get a Roommate

You may already have a roommate picked out. It could be someone you are already friends with or a teammate. Alternatively, you may not have a clue who you will room with. This can be nerve wracking because you will be moving in with someone you do not know and hoping it will work out. The residence life staff does their best to match students with similar likes but they do not get it right all of the time.

With that in mind, you will most definitely meet fellow incoming first year students during orientation that you could make a connection with. If you do, you can request to be roommates and while you will not be close friends when you move in, you will have a leg up because you do know the person and feel you are compatible enough to room together.

For those who request roommates or for those who are assigned roommates, you can do something prior to arriving in fall. It would be smart to connect with your roommate via email, phone or in person and try to get to know them before you arrive. It is also smart because you can decide who is going to bring what to the room (i.e. you really do not need two refrigerators). Sabrina, a sophomore, told me that she went out for coffee with her assigned roommate and it made all the difference in the world. They felt that they knew each other well enough to make the move-in day fun and something to look forward to.

Housing Registration

Many colleges set aside a time to register for housing. This includes any preference of a roommate and residence hall. In my experience, most students do not take a campus map with them when completing tours and rarely ask about residence halls that are preferred by students. Remember, think about where the residence hall is in relation to where most of your classes will be, where the cafeteria is, and where other services you will use (i.e. athletic fields, student center) are located. The weather may not always cooperate and a shorter walk to class may be attractive to you.

Meet Athletic Staff and Fellow Athletes

If you have declared your intent to play a NCAA sport while at college, there will certainly be times scheduled to meet the athletic staff of your chosen sport. You will also meet other incoming athletes at these meetings. Meeting your teammates before the semester begins can help you immensely. At the very least, you may find a roommate that you can communicate and coordinate with before heading out to school in August. You can figure out what each of you will contribute to the room and you can become friends before August (again, creating important connections).

Get Your Syllabi From Your Professors

This may seem like odd advice because you do not have the professor yet but hear me out on this one. Many schools post old syllabi online for you to see. You can get an understanding of what you will learn and what will be expected of you, like tests, papers and readings. The only problem is that most professors will not have their fall syllabi complete until much closer to the semester. So, once you know which courses you're going to be in and who is going to teach them, contact that professor and ask for an old syllabus (but the most recent one) for the class. The dates will be off and the professor will probably make some changes but it is likely that the books and readings will stay the same. You should ask just to make sure. By doing this, you could actually buy the books and start reading.

This may not sound like a fantastic summer activity but it will have major benefits for you once you arrive. First, you will have done the reading. After that, all that you will need to do is skim and review once the actual reading is due. Second, this gives you more time to do work in other classes. Third, you will be able contribute in class from the first day because you have worked ahead. As a side note, I always give this advice to those who are planning to go to law school because they will be working 10 hours a day every day of the week during their first year. Why not decrease your workload by getting ahead?

I definitely practice what I preach here. In summer, I try to work just a few hours a day on syllabi, prepping out my classes, reading, or even writing this book. I make sure my syllabi are printed out and on my desk when I walk in the door the first day of classes. I do not work eight-hour days five days a week because its summer, but I work a little every day so I can go into my fall semester with less stress. It works like a champ.

Conclusion

Orientations vary among different colleges. They will vary in relation to timing since some have spring orientations, some have summer orientations, and some even have a longer pre-class fall orientation. Some colleges make the early orientations optional rather than mandatory but you should not let that dissuade you from attending. Orientations will even vary in relation to what you actually do when you are there. The advice given above continues to hold true – Regardless of timing, length, attendance options, or activities, the goal is for you to attend and make the most out of it. Even if you do not accomplish all the tasks listed above, you need to attend and be an active participant.

Perhaps I can put the importance of attending into context. When you moved up from middle to high school, you were likely nervous on your first day to high school. But think back. You worked your way up through middle school and likely began to understand how to survive school life at the tail end of your first year. By the last year of middle school, you were likely comfortable about how to navigate, study and survive in a way that worked for you. The same holds true for the transition to high school and the transition to college.

Think about how much easier that transition to high school would have been if you had attended a day or two of orientation and completed some of the activities I listed above. At the very least, high school would have been demystified and the transition much less drastic. You still would have experienced a transition, just as if you will when you go to college, but it simply becomes smoother when you have an idea of what to expect. This analogy holds true for a new job or car, marriage, or even the death of someone

89

close to you. You still have to experience it but the
impact is lessened.

Your First Semester

Introduction

You have moved through the whole process of researching, visiting, and choosing your college. You may have found this to be very time consuming and it may have involved a great deal of travel. After all of your visits, you made the choice. You have also been communicating with your college over the course of the summer and have visited for your orientation(s). Now it is time to pack up and go. This is it!

You may be excited, nervous, or both. You will definitely have some anxiety and it is completely normal. For almost everyone, this is likely the biggest and most significant change you have undergone in your life and because of that, nerves and anxiety levels will be high. You may be thinking of the fact that you are going away to college with few or no friends that you know. You may be thinking of your sport and how college athletics are going to be different. You may wonder how you are going to get involved or if you will succeed at academics. The point is this: Your mind will be swirling around with all the questions that you will not have answers to until you get there and start experiencing first hand. You cannot really know what college is like until you get there. The information in the previous chapters should help ease your pain somewhat but there is no substitute for experience, and this is it.

This chapter will start with some basic but extremely important information that should follow you through your college career. After, the chapter will be organized chronologically. I will first address your first two weeks at college followed by a discussion revolving around the middle of the semester. Lastly. I will speak to the end of the semester and the importance of finishing strong.

Important Information to Consider When You Arrive

Many new college students leave the college they are at during their first semester, right after their first semester, or in between their first and second year. In fact, the retention rates (percentage of first year college students who return to the same college for their sophomore year) range from a high of 99% to a low of less than 50%. On average, about one out of three students do not return to college the next year and that is a shocking statistic to me. (Smith-Barrow, 2016)

Students leave for a variety of reasons. These reasons are related to academics (lack of preparation, disinterest or boredom), motivation (low levels of commitment, perceived irrelevance of the college experience), psychosocial causes (social factors, emotional factors) and financial reasons (too expensive, perception that the cost of college outweighs the benefits). There are no magic words that I can give about the increasing cost of college but I hope my words here can help ease the stress of the transition and help you succeed in those other areas. Every faculty and staff member wants you to be successful in college. We are on your side and will help you but the ball is in your court. Your success depends wholly on you. My hope with this chapter is to give you information so you have a better idea what you are getting into and as I have said before, the more knowledge you have beforehand, the better off you will be.

Making Connections

Much of what colleges try to do is to keep you at that college until you get your degree and a great deal of that work starts with the incoming first year class. To help increase their retention rate, colleges bring in the first year class early, sometimes well before the returning students come back. At the college where I teach, first year students arrive on campus three days before returning students do. Colleges do this because they know that the struggle acclimating to college life is something that most first years go through and easing that transition is very important. We do not want you coming in August and leaving in September or October. If you feel connected (whatever that means for you) to that particular college, you will be less likely to transfer.

At pre-semester orientation, you will certainly make connections with other first year students because that is the primary goal. You will learn about the college, participate in many icebreakers and get valuable information that can help keep you out of trouble. You will also make connections with upper class students, fellow athletes, your roommate, orientation leaders and resident assistants (R.A's), and even faculty. You will also meet your neighbors and that will help because you will definitely need them for more things than you could know. All of the activities you do during this period will have a function related to your success at the college you are attending. In short, you could be the smartest person on the block but that does not make it more likely that you will stay at college – We want you to be part of the college community and have a support system. That is what keeps you in college!

You will likely have several ice-breaking sessions at orientation. In these sessions, you will complete activities that will help you get to know the other students. These may seem goofy and slightly embarrassing at times but they really do work. They allow you the opportunity to be a bit vulnerable by doing something embarrassing. That opens up others in the group to you and you to them because you are all doing it. These ice-breaking sessions work. So, while you may not think that they are cool, they will help you get a group of friends much quicker than you would be able to on your own.

You are also going to spend some time learning about student conduct code. This usually revolves around two primary topics. The first topic is about drinking and using drugs. The second topic focuses on sexual assault and consent. It would be smart for you to find the college's online student handbook and know all of their conduct policies. Even if you do not do the research, you will definitely hear about them before you start classes, probably on the day you arrive.

Alcohol and Drug Use

In relation to alcohol and drugs, many schools have very strict policies. They work diligently at reducing the amount of alcohol and drug use on campus and policies reflect that desire. Here is the gist of it with alcohol. If you are under 21, then you cannot possess alcohol. Period. You can be charged with a student conduct code violation and some schools will even charge you with possession of empty alcohol bottles, so do not display them as a badge of honor or as candleholders. In some schools, you can be charged with misconduct under the influence of alcohol. For example, you can be charged if someone has to call the ambulance because of your over-drinking, even if you do not possess any alcohol at all. In relation to being

95

intoxicated, you cannot be charged with that *unless* your behavior is problematic. You should not drink but if you choose to, either do it off campus (and do not drive) or keep quiet in your room so you do not give an excuse for the R.A's to come knocking on your door. In short, there is nothing that will get you in trouble more than being stupid when you are drunk. Life decisions have consequences and whatever you choose to do, understand that any consequences that you incur will be of your own making and no one else's.

In relation to drugs, the policies and conduct code are usually very strict, much more so than alcohol. Many schools will suspend you upon your first drug possession charge and if they do not on the first, they will likely do it on the second. The amount of drugs you have is much less relevant than the fact that you possess them unless you are dealing drugs. Dealing is the quickest way to be suspended or expelled from college and you will likely be immediately arrested. Moreover, if you are in a residence hall room and there are several of you who are doing drugs, all will get charged, even those who were not actually partaking. If they are in the room and cannot prove who was smoking or who possessed it, everyone will get charged. You should not do drugs but if you choose to, do them off campus, be safe about it, and do not drive.

A final note on drug use. You may think you are slick by toweling the door or covering the smoke detector in your residence hall room. Toweling just does not work and if you cover the smoke detector, you will get charged with both drugs and fire safety violations and I would bet that the penalty for covering the smoke detector might be as harsh as the penalty for drugs. If they come knocking on your door because they smell smoke, you may think you are smart by throwing your drugs or paraphernalia out the window.

What you may be forgetting is that college administrations have been encountering this problem for years and know all the tricks. They may even have an R.A. waiting under your window with a baseball glove and know that the college security department will have the police on speed dial if they are not sworn officers themselves.

While you may not find this next advice appealing, it might be smart to do a little research anyway. I can almost guarantee that you will experience drunk people in the residence halls. Some will be very drunk to the point that they need care. You may want to do a bit of research on how to take care of them. You may feel that it is not your job but it is because you are human. All I can say is please be careful and take care of those around you that need help and be sure to know who to call for help (i.e. ambulance). Please be sure to read the relevant sections of your college's student handbook in regard to drug and alcohol use because the college will assume that you have.

Sexual Assault on Campus

Sexual assault is more prevalent than you think. I will not spend too much time talking about it but I will say that is a problem. While forcible rapes do occur on college campuses around the country, what does occur much more often is sex after drinking? Inhibitions go down as the desire for sex increases. What you have to understand (and this relates to both males and females) is that if a female is under the influence of alcohol (or drugs), she *cannot* legally consent. A male student could get verbal permission, written permission and even video permission and it still will not equal consent. What this means is that in

97

most states and at many colleges, sex while drunk fully qualifies as a sexual assault, which you can be suspended, expelled and even arrested for. If you are arrested for it, you may end up in the sex offender database – which is for life. For males, there is no better way to ruin your life and future employment and relationships than being a registered sex offender. For females, no one should have to bear the scars of a sexual assault. Please be sure to read the relevant sections of your college's student handbook in regard to sexual assault because the college will assume that you have.

Consequences of Bad Behavior

You are going to start experiencing freedom that most of you have never had and this will start on the first day of college. There are no curfews or parents to watch over you and limit you. You have the full ability to have as much fun as you want. Just know that the choices that you make have serious and possibly lifelong consequences. These are your choices to make.

In those first days after you are dropped off, it is very important for you to listen and understand the policies the college staff speaks to you about. They will be written in the student handbook for you to read as well. You are an adult now and must make adult choices and not knowing will not be an excuse. In college, your adult choices have adult consequences. The first few days are going to be important for you to make friends but also to understand the rules. Pre-class orientation helps toward this goal. Please listen intently and if you do not understand something, ask your orientation leader or an R.A. Someone else likely has the same question as you.

If you end up getting charged with a violation of the student conduct code, there are some steps you need to take. First, answer all emails or contact requests made by the college in a very timely fashion (less than one day). When you meet with a college representative for the first time, you may want to ask for an advocate or someone who knows the system, who can guide you through the process. This can be a staff or faculty member, or sometimes a student. This person will serve as the 'defense attorney' although their role is more about making sure you understand the process than actually 'defending' you.

If you are factually responsible, if you did what they are accusing you of doing, you need to act like an adult and take responsibility. More often than not, you will be found responsible and it can only work to your benefit if you take responsibility rather than deny it and be later found guilty. While college staff members do not want to give out harsh penalties, it is likely that the penalty will be harsher if you deny responsibility. As I have spoken to in many places in this book, be an adult and act like an adult. If you make a mistake, own up to it, move on, and learn from your mistakes. If you choose not to, you may want to be very familiar with the student conduct code and the penalty system your college uses.

Your Hygiene

Lastly, a topic that will likely not be brought up during orientation deserves brief mention here. Keeping yourself clean is extremely important. Please work very hard not to fall behind on your laundry or showering because we can tell and it is not pretty for anyone. This may sound harsh but no one likes when you smell.

The First Two Weeks

When you get to college, you will likely still feel like you are a high school student because that is all you have experienced. You will soon realize that this is not the case. While Chapter 3 focused on the differences between high school and college, you will not really know just how different college is until you experience it once classes begin.

The first two weeks are going to be crucial for you. They will set the tone in regard to how your semester is going to play out. If you start with good habits, they will likely remain and get stronger. If you start by slacking, it is likely either you will have to work your tail off to catch up or you will be going home. Below are a few tips that can help start the semester off nicely.

My best advice is to start thinking about your grade now rather than at the end of the semester. Many students just push along and do average work and then realize that they have to work three times as hard at the end of the semester to get a good grade. Be committed at the beginning of the semester and in the end, you may have some breathing room. For example, I exempt students from the final exam in most of my courses if they have an 'A' average. I push them to work hard the entire semester then give them the gift of not having to take my final exam. Even if your professor does not offer that option, start committing on day one and you will have much less stress during finals.

Go to All of Your Classes

I know this may sound silly but your first task is to go to your classes...all of them. You do not want to start your first semester of college behind and if you begin to miss classes, that is what will happen. It is so important to attend all your classes the first two weeks because that is when professors describe what will happen in the course while at the same time, letting you understand who they are and their expectations. Your task is to intentionally listen and watch, not act out. Acting out or working as hard as you can to become the center of attention or the coolest kid in class will not go over well with the professor and other students. You can learn much more than class content when you go and listen. You will learn by watching other students, especially those who are returning students and those who have had that professor in a previous class. Much can be learned from students who are taking a second or third class from the same professor because they know how they can behave and they know what will be expected from them. So, during those first few weeks, go to class and while there, look, learn and listen. You will gain valuable experience toward how college students should act in class.

I've had more than my share of experiences when first years are acting out, especially when they are in a first year seminar course and all of the students in the class are first years. I have had them not listen, act out toward other students and act out toward me. Make no mistake, when those events happen, I quietly let them know that they need to come to my office and the resulting 'chat' will not end well. Just work hard not to put yourself in that position because to be honest, I am a very relaxed and easygoing professor but when you disrespect me or another student, I get a bit cranky and we will have a conversation. While that

101

conversation will be calm and informative, *you will know* what you can and cannot do in my classes. Unfortunately, I cannot guarantee how other professors will respond in the same situation and it may not be as calm.

Don't Drop Any Classes (unless there is an overriding need to)

Sounds like silly advice again but it happens all the time. Many students drop classes when they realize that they either do not like the class (or professor) or feel that they have fallen behind. Remember, your first semester is a bit of a crapshoot. In other words, you have little experience with what you are going to take and whom you are going to take it from. After this semester, you can ask for guidance from other students in relation to what professors to take classes from.

With that in mind, it is smart to push through your first semester and stick with all your classes for several reasons. First, this will not be the last time you take classes you do not want to take. Sticking with it will help you succeed in later classes that you are not excited about. Second, it will help you with time management and limit your free time. You are going to have a good deal of free time even with a full load of classes but you do not want too much free time. More free hours could lead to more socializing, and while that is not a bad thing, it can lead to the avoidance of work and attendance issues in your other courses. Third, you do not want to fall behind on credits in the first semester. While it can be easy to make up credits over the course of a few semesters or summer semester, you want to avoid falling behind. Lastly, your parents will not be happy. You can imagine how they might feel if you are throwing their money away, which is what dropping a class essentially becomes. They probably will not be getting their money back.

That being said, there might be circumstances where you absolutely must drop but this decision should not be related to how you feel about the class. Instead, it should only be related to whether you feel overloaded with work. The hardest thing about being overloaded with work in college is that by the time you understand you have too much to do and are stressed, you are much further behind than you realize. Many realize it much too late. So, if you are keeping track of yourself and your work and you recognize that the stress is too much, then go ahead and drop a class. It will not be the worst decision ever if you use the extra time for the classes you are staying with.

If you have to drop a class to avoid an F, just make sure to think about it and speak to your advisor. While you do not want to start college behind in credits, there are benefits to dropping. First, if you do it early enough, you will end up with a 'W' or withdrawal on your academic transcript rather than an F. Withdrawals do not impact your G.P.A., but the F will. Second, not dropping could actually facilitate lower grades in your other classes because you are either spending too much time on the troubling class or worried by the fact that you are doing badly. Both of these will likely impact your other courses. Third, by dropping, you would have more time to do better in your other courses, if you choose to use your time wisely. On a final note, if you do drop, colleges usually have a one or two-week window where the class will not show up on your transcript and you have the ability to add another class in its place. Keep in mind that you will be starting that course a week or two behind.

Balance your Socializing with your Academics

Freedom is a lovely thing. With no parents or other adults to watch over you, the sky is the limit. You may find that you are indulging in that freedom a bit too much. If in the first two weeks, you are not going to classes, not going to bed until very late, sleeping until the afternoon, or over-indulging in alcohol or drug use, you are going to be in trouble. If this is the case, you will likely be back home before the end of the semester. You will fall behind quickly and that is not the way to start your first semester. As I noted in the above section, you should be smart when deciding how much partying and socializing you are doing. I am a realist and after over twenty years teaching college, I know better than to mandate that you avoid socializing since it is an important part of your college experience and your learning. That being said, I will advise that you temper just how much socializing you do until you get a better idea of how much you can manage. One final note: During the first two weekends of college, the campus life staff will be extra diligent with a watchful eye for drugs and alcohol and many first year students will be written up and charged with violating the substance policies. Do not be one of those students who goes home in those first two weeks.

Being Homesick

You and many of your friends may get homesick during those first two weeks of college and beyond. It is ok and very normal. The problem is that homesickness expresses itself in various ways. In other words, being homesick doesn't necessarily mean that you're crying on your bed missing your parents, friends, boyfriend or girlfriend, or your dog (by the way, if you're a dog lover and see one on campus, go pet it. You will be happy you did). You may see that you are becoming angry or short-tempered when you usually are not. You may notice that you are overindulging in alcohol. Homesickness can impact your sleep patterns, and it can impact both your attendance in your classes and the work you choose to submit or not submit.

I have only a few pieces of advice here. First, work to recognize what you are feeling and find a way to speak to a friend or family member about it. If you are angry because your roommate left their shoes on your side of the room, it is a good chance that you are not mad about the shoes. It is more likely that you are having transition problems and you are not able to see the real sources of your stress. Those first two weeks can be very difficult but if you work to recognize what you are feeling, it allows you a buffer zone between what you are truly feeling and behaviors that may arise because of those feelings. So recognizing what is going on and having someone to talk with is important. I have had students come in my office crying uncontrollably because they were struggling so much with the transition to college and being homesick. Remember, this is likely the most significant life change for most of you and you have to find a way to deal with the impact of it. Colleges have great counseling centers and if you want to speak with someone confidentially who has experience in this area, the counseling center is the place to go. Talk to your advisor, friend, roommate or whomever you can express yourself to. Go outside and get some sun. Whatever you do, take time out of your day to relax in the way you like to relax.

Second, and this may sound odd, do not go home in the first two weeks. To be honest, you should not go home during the first six weeks. Do not do it.

105

Do not even think about it. First, you are not doing yourself any favors by going home because after a short weekend, any homesickness you have will be prolonged over the course of the semester. You will come back feeling more homesick and you may even go home more often. This only keeps those homesick feelings in the forefront of your mind.

Also, you will miss out on a crucial period of forming connections and friendships during those first few weeks while others are making friends and getting close. If there is anything that will help reduce those feelings of homesickness, making friends will do it. So, in those first two weeks, work as hard as you can to make those friends and connections because it will help and you will end up with an immediate support group.

Start Learning How to Study

If you skip class, avoid studying, fail to read the material, take poor notes, zone out in class, or cram, you will not do well on tests. Cramming for tests *does not work* and is counterproductive. You may have done this in high school and it may have worked for you but it will be less likely to work for you in college. You are going to have to cram at some point but know that it is not even close to the best and most efficient way to study. I will talk more about good study skills in the next chapter but know that you are going to have to re-learn how to study. Now is the time to think about it because with only eight semesters, you want good habits to start as early as possible.

Midterms and Beyond

Start Finding your Place

You are going to find that the quiet place in your bedroom at home may be gone. You are going to have a roommate who you may or may not know, your residence hall will be far from quiet, and you will find that there is always someone around. In short, you could find that your room may not be the best place to find quiet and time for yourself.

With this in mind, you will need to find a place where you can be alone and you will want to find one for a few reasons. First, alone time helps calm you down, especially if you are struggling with the transition to college. Second, you will need a place to study where you can be productive. I will speak more to studying and reading in Chapter 6 but suffice it to say, you will need to find a space that works for you.

For alone time, get outside and take a walk. The sun and breeze can do wonders. Even your room can be a good place to be alone. Get your roommate's class schedule so you know the times you can be alone. Also, lock your door and put on headphones so you are not tempted to answer the door when someone comes knocking. Go to the gym and work out. I am not asking you to be anti-social. Instead, I am asking that you be good to yourself during a time when you may find the need to escape or get away.

For a place to be productive, you will find that college buildings have many nooks and crannies for private studying. Students think that the library is where they should go to study and that is a great place because they are there to facilitate reading and studying. Even though this is true, more and more college libraries are academic gathering places rather than the quiet library scene one imagines. You can even bring food and drink into many libraries now. Instead, think about the student centers on campus because after the dining halls close, the number of students in there will decrease substantially. Think about finding an academic building and classrooms that are not occupied. Think about a coffee shop or diner far enough from campus that you will not be tempted to socialize with other students. College campuses have many places to study that are not always associated with studying. Wander around a bit and find what works for you.

Don't Fall Behind

The minute you think you are falling behind, you already are. You are likely a few weeks behind. I am very serious here. It starts with missing an assignment or two that you may or may not make up. Procrastination can lead to avoiding your big term paper or other assignments. You may have crammed for a test or two. All of these are indicators that you are falling behind and if there is one thing for certain in college, as the semester wears on, it becomes more and more difficult to catch up. Think about it this way: You will be busier in September than in August. You will be busier in October than in September. By the time you get to the end of the semester, the work compounds and with final exams and large term papers due, life will get very busy. Finals are not fun for anyone but walking into final exams behind in your classes will lead to a very high probability that you will not do as well. When catching up, you are losing sleep and focus, and the work product will certainly suffer. Work as hard as you can at submitting your work when it's due and complete your reading before class. Do your homework, please do your homework!

For me, I let students turn in work as late as they want but I take a letter grade off every day that it is late. I make very few exceptions and I do not give extensions. So, for me, be as late as you want but you will know the penalties that you will incur. You really only have one job as a college student and all we ask is for you to do it.

Start Thinking About Your Spring Courses

I know you are still reeling a bit because it is your first semester but there is no time like the present to start thinking about your spring classes. You will likely be advised and start to register for spring around the beginning of November but you do not want to wait that long before thinking about this. Remember that as first year students, you will register last and your choices may not be as desirable.

It would be smart to approach your spring semester schedule as you did for your fall schedule. Focus on taking a class or two for your major, some general education requirements, and a one or two credit class to bulk up on credits. As I said in the last chapter, speak to professors whose courses you think will fill up before you have a chance to register and get on their wait list. We love when students do that because it shows that you are excited and interested! If you work hard in advance, that work will pay off. If you do not, you will likely get a schedule you hate that includes early morning and Friday classes. This is very avoidable though, so take advantage of the opportunity to start planning early.

Now that you are starting to get the hang of scheduling, I want to add one more piece of advice.

Try to make your schedule such that you do not have more than three classes in one day and no more than two classes in a row. If you have more than three classes in a day, that day will be awful for you because you'll have homework for each class due on the same day (and likely tests and big papers as well). You will also be exhausted because four classes in a day is a lot. You do not want more than two in a row because your mind needs time to recharge. If my class was your third in a row, I would be able to tell very quickly because you would not have the attention or motivation. Your mind needs its breaks. This also gives you time to get some food in you and perhaps take a quick nap. Don't skip lunch, ok?

Get Involved and Continue to Balance Your Time

All colleges have clubs that you can join. They range from student government to intramural sports to outdoors and camping clubs. You will be able to go online, usually under the student life pages, and see what organizations you can join. The benefit is that you will gain more friends who have the same interests as you.

On the other side of the coin, try not to join too many organizations. If you are extroverted or just want to be involved in as much as you can, it can be dangerous to over-commit yourself. What I have found is that the organizations you join will be excited about your excitement and will want you to do more and more for them. Couple that with more than one or two organizations and your time will be taken away from your schoolwork very quickly. Your stress levels will also rise because you will start falling behind on your work while at the same time, working to not disappoint the members of your group. That will lead

110

to spending more time on organization business than schoolwork. Just be stingy with your time, no one will blame you.

Who You Absolutely Need to Know Well

There are four people that you need to get to know well at college. I am sure there are more but in my opinion, these folks are the top four. By getting to know and making a connection with each of these people, your college career will likely become easier. You should introduce yourself by name to each of these people and go out of your way to stop, say hello, and make a bit of conversation unrelated to any needs that you might have.

Know your housekeeper. They are in the trenches, so to speak, and rarely get accolades for their hard work. They likely are not paid enough and are not really noticed. Get to know them well. When I lived in the residence halls, I found out that my housekeeper liked drinking a specific soda so I bought a 12 pack every other week for her. She was very appreciative and for a few dollars out of my pocket, I made a connection and had the cleanest bathroom on campus! Do not, under any circumstances, assume that the housekeeper is your personal maid. Also, do not make huge messes in your bathroom and leave them for the housekeeper. Their job is to keep the campus clean but it should not be their job to clean up after a student's inconsiderate behavior. Again, this is another piece of advice that revolves around being a respectful and accountable adult.

Know your advisor. Your academic advisor is the one that helps guide you through your college years and helps you move toward graduation in the best way they know how. Understand that they will know more than you will and will have valuable advice. Understand that their time is busy so you want to respect that by doing your job and coming prepared to meetings. You will also want to stop by occasionally to say hello and ask how they are doing. By making a connection with your advisor and doing your job as a student, it makes them want to help you more compared to being a student who is unprepared and expects immediate assistance at the last second. This is never something you want to do and unfortunately, it happens way too often.

Know a specific person in the registrar's office and another in the student financial accounts office. The registrar's office has control over the class schedule and registration for those classes and any drops or adds you want to make. The student financial aid and accounts office has control over the student accounts, financial aid, and at times, scholarships. Rarely do these staff members get a kind word from students and instead, students come in and demand a great deal. Staff in these offices see disgruntled students often, especially when the student financial aid refund checks do not come in on time. By being friendly, saying hello when you don't need anything from them, you might just get service with a smile and better attention than someone who comes in mad and demanding (like the old saying goes, you get more flies with honey than vinegar).

Finishing Strong

You have made it through most of the semester and that is great news. The bad news is that life is going to get busy very quickly. You are going to have a ton of work at the end of the semester. Finals will be looming and you will feel the pressure to do well to end up with a good grade in the class. You will have one or several large term papers due all around the same date. You will still have reading, homework and quizzes. When added up together, you are going to be busy and stressed.

My advice here is simple. I want you to work your tail off to finish strong. It is going to be stressful and you are probably not going to like it but the work is not going to go away. You might have worked all semester or you might have procrastinated. Those that worked hard all semester will have it easier but it will still be stressful because everyone around you is pressured and wherever you go on campus, everyone will be uptight (in residence halls, cafeteria, library, classrooms). Regardless of what category you are in, make the effort to complete your work. It is not going to disappear so figure out a way to finish it and have it be the best product you can submit.

I do not mean to push doom and gloom but I want you to understand how stressful it will be. You can do it! Those before you have done it and those after you will. Be confident that you can and you will be able to take control and get your work done. I promise!

Conclusion

Once you have started college your first semester, it all comes down to you. It is your education and for you to succeed, you have to learn how to become a college student. In other words, you have to do your job because professors will not do it for you. I cannot emphasize this more. By adopting some or all of the techniques I have given you here, you can make that transition to being a college student a bit easier and can set yourself up for success later. Start strong, be consistent and finish strong. Good habits obtained early can make a world of difference.

Being an Effective & Efficient Student - Academics

Introduction

There are many books that can help guide you toward success in college. The goal with this book is for you to learn and practice the skills needed to succeed - starting early in your college career. If you are reading this, you should begin practicing these skills while still in high school. I may sound like a broken record here but if you can begin learning and practicing college level behavior (academic or otherwise); it will be much easier for you once you finally arrive at college.

This chapter will focus on helping you become a more effective <u>and</u> efficient college student. I will speak to academics and studying, as many books do, but I will also speak to non-academic skills and techniques that will support your academic work. My goal is to give you skills so you can be efficient at what you do. The more efficient you are, the more effective you will be. The more effective you are, the stronger the work product, whether in college, a summer job, at home, or after college. This chapter will focus primarily on the academic side of being an efficient student and the next chapter will focus on the administrative side.

Please understand that there are several sources in print and on the web that can help guide you toward academic success and what I have written below will not be the complete list of how to succeed. What I have written below focuses on my experience as a college professor for two decades and what I have seen work and not work. <u>Remember, the techniques you use to succeed may work for you but not the person next to you.</u> We all we learn differently. My hope is that you read this important information and take with you what will work for you, and perhaps try something new. I know these techniques work because I have seen them succeed repeatedly but what you choose to adopt is solely up to you.

Tests

Tests: Studying

a. When to Study

There are functional and nonfunctional ways of studying. Cramming for an examination the night before is a *nonfunctional* way of studying. You may be saying to yourself that it worked for you in high school so why bother changing now? The answer is that college is not the same as high school. There is little spoon-feeding in college and you are expected to know and be able to apply the information even if you did not go over it in class. It is more than just rote memorization. Anyone can memorize a definition given the appropriate amount of time, but if you cannot give an example or apply it to a relevant situation; you cannot say that you really know what it means.

This section starts with the golden rule: Do not cram for tests. You will learn less and you will not score as high on tests compared to using techniques that are more functional. Sabrina, a sophomore, said that she didn't feel as comfortable or do nearly as well on any test when she crammed compared to when she stretched the studying out over three or four days. Keep this in mind and below you will find techniques that will work if you choose to employ them.

If you start studying a week or two or even five days before the examination, you will likely score higher than if you cram the night before. To put it bluntly, you can only force-feed your brain (like your stomach) so much at a sitting. Learning over time allows your brain to rest and recuperate. Most of what we learn is done over time. In this scenario, you will want to use the technique that works for you but I strongly recommend doing a certain amount of studying every single day leading up to the test. If it takes you one hour to read your notes or work through your flashcards, do that every day leading up to the test. If you are starting a week before the test, you will have studied for seven hours, and all without cramming or pulling an all-nighter.

If we take the above suggestion a step further, one of the most functional ways to study, and more importantly, retain the material and score well on tests, is to start after the first class. Here is how starting on the first day can really help you study efficiently. Read the material before the class and take notes on it. Bring those notes to class and use them to supplement the notes that you take in class. If you can put both sets of notes on the same sheets, all the better. In itself, that is just getting ready for class but here is where it becomes functional for studying.

Once you get back from class, type up your notes from class and from the book. Again, it would be better if you could put both sets of notes together because that shows you can synthesize the information but if you only end up typing up the lecture notes, it's better than nothing. Now, read the typed notes you just finished.

On the second day of class, do the same thing except you will want to read the notes from both the first and second day of class. On the third day do the same thing except you want to read notes from the first, second and third day of class. If you think about it, it is less studying and more about reviewing because you are literally reviewing after every class. By the time the test comes, you may hardly have to study at all because you have been doing it already for several weeks. This technique takes the most commitment but yields the best results.

There is an important thing to consider here. If you have read your notes and you do not understand something, go ask your professor about it so you can get clarification early. I would also bring your notes to the professor and see what they say about their accuracy and organization. Are you hitting or missing the big points? Are your notes organized? Did you write something down in error? If you do this early on, it will help you in that class and others as well.

I guarantee that these techniques will work but in all honesty, it is likely that at some point in your college career, and likely in your first semester, you will find yourself needing to cram for a test. When I asked Rebekah, a recent graduate, about cramming, here is what she said: "I completely agree with the no cramming advice. It's a safety net that some freshman fall victim to during the first year, and some stick with this study habit for all four years not realizing there are better, more efficient ways to learn while in college." With that being said, some of the first year classes may feel like high-school classes because they are introductory and they are 'easy.' For example, if you take an introductory course that is easy and you already have some knowledge in the subject area, you may be able to successfully cram the day before that test.

This is where students can fall victim to feeling it's okay to cram. Be aware that for the more challenging courses, cramming will not work. You need to begin to develop and learn your study habits early and applying those techniques to the early classes can help later on. Rebekah also said, "Cramming is better than not studying at all! Sorry to say, but sometimes you gotta do what you gotta do to get by. Freshmen have the tendency to learn as they go because they are unsure what path is better. If you do not learn early that cramming is not the best way to go, it is still a way to go (if that makes sense). Not saying that cramming is good, but it is better than nothing."

My advice is not to cram for tests. If, however, you do find yourself short of time and you have to spend a great deal of time studying the night before the test, you will want to study for a certain period of time and then take a break. Studying for thirty minutes and taking a ten-minute break is a good place to start. Go outside and get some fresh air – no social media or YouTube. However, I would avoid studying for more than thirty minutes before taking break. Given that your short on time, you need to make the most of your studying and taking regular breaks can help you stay focused when you need to be.

b. Where to Study

As I noted in an earlier chapter, you need to find your place at your college. This means how you fit in and whom you fit in with, but it also means literally finding a place that you can study that works for you. Whether that is your room, a local coffee shop, an academic building, or the library, it is crucial to find a place where you can concentrate and get your work done with little distraction. I used to study in my dorm room with the radio on but only playing static. It sounds weird but I played it just loud enough so the white noise drowned out everything going on outside my room. You may not figure out the best place to study for a semester or two but it will come.

c. Who to Study With

When you are considering who to study with, it may mean no one, but in some classes, you may find it more functional to study with a small group of others or a close friend from the class. Small study groups can be wonderful because learning information from a different person allows you the chance to understand what you might not have before. Small groups can also be a fun way to re-learn the material for an exam. The same principles about cramming hold true, however. Cramming with a small group the night before will not be as functional as having a regular meeting time before the test. Also, work hard not to get distracted with side conversations.

d. What to Study

Is this going to be on the test? Is this important? I hear these questions often right before tests and certainly in review sessions. I always give the same answer to both questions – "Yes!" If I taught it and if you read it, it is important. That being said, not everything can show up on the tests and while you may be able to predict what is going to be asked on an exam, it is a risky proposition to put all your eggs in one basket. Below is some general advice that can help narrow down what the professor will likely test you on.

Before moving on, you have to understand that testing methods and what you will have to prove on tests will change as you move forward with your college career. In your first year, the tests for your lower level classes will have a stronger memorization component. There will be some application and some essays but for the most part, you will get many short answer and multiple-choice tests. As you move toward your junior and senior year, you will be expected to dig much deeper. You will get more essay exams and some exams that will be take home papers. Do not be surprised, however, if you find yourself doing more writing on exams early on in your college career. Just be prepared.

Exams get progressively more complex because you should be able to make stronger theoretical and practical connections with your growth as a college student. This should not scare you, but you need to be prepared. In my upper level courses, I regularly give a ten-page paper as a final exam that has only one question and that is cumulative in nature. This type of testing would be so difficult for incoming first years but less so for upper class students. I am telling you this now because it changes how you will study for exams as you move forward. You will be thinking more about the material and making connections compared to rote memorization as you move to your junior and senior years. Below are some tips that can help.

First, if the professor writes it on the board, you should study it. If a professor impresses upon you that it would be smart to take notes on a particular piece of information, it is important. That being said, in some classes, the smaller things are also important. For example, you will likely have to remember specific dates and names of artists in an art history class. In an anatomy class, you will likely have to know all of the bones in the body. In a criminal justice class, however, dates and specific names will be less important than the laws or theories. In my policing class, how discretion works is ultimately more important than the date of the first modern police force (1829 in London, if you were wondering).

If there are items that show up in the book *and* are ones that the professor discusses in class, they will likely be on the test. This information will be more important than something you read that is not discussed in class. Keep in mind that there is always a chance that information that you read but that is not discussed in class will be on the test. My tests are based more on the lecture than the reading but I always put one or two questions on my tests from the book that I may not have reviewed in class. Missing one or two questions may not sound that detrimental but that could result in a half or full letter grade score lower. The point is that you should focus your studying on the more important information but not forget to review what you consider the less important information.

Asking other students who have had that particular professor before what those professors look for with their tests is something that happens often. There is an upside and downside to doing this. The upside is that you can get an idea of the types of questions that a professor asks on their exams. The downside is that many students focus their studying on what the other student told them. This can be both unpredictable and problematic. You just never know what or how that other person studies so if you rely on a student who took the class before, you do so at your own risk.

In my courses, I put the learning objectives of the particular class session on the board prior to the start of class. It lets students know how we are going to proceed that day and what I want to cover. By doing so, I have told them clearly what is important to learn that day. Not only that, I have also given them a review sheet they can start working with from the very first day of class. Not all professors do this but it would not be a bad idea to literally train your professors by asking them, every day, what the learning objectives of the class session are. If you start doing that in all your classes, everyone, including you, will benefit greatly.

e. Why Study

You have to study to do well. How much may vary among different learners but you will need to spend time studying. You may think that because you came to class, you will do fine on the exam, but that is not always the case. In fact, I have taught many smart students who do poorly on tests because they did not study. This over-confidence can get you in trouble and by the time you learn that lesson (after a bad grade on the first test), you have put yourself in a hole and making a good grade in the class becomes more difficult. Start early and study often by treating school like a job and the learning will happen. You will also learn that studying works and that builds confidence in both your study skills and test taking.

f. How to Study

I have addressed this in the above sections but there is an important point that I want to touch on again. You may feel that your technique works and if it does, hone the skill. I would not want to advise you to try something completely different but it may be beneficial to incorporate a suggestion or two that I have made into your studying regime. It may help. On the other hand, if you do not score well on tests, it is likely due to either not studying enough or studying the wrong information. If you do not spend enough time studying, only you can make that change and make studying a priority. If you found that you studied the wrong information, get your study materials together and bring them to the professor to look at and assess. I cannot tell you how many times I would look at completely disorganized notebooks and flashcards with the wrong answers on them. We have office hours for a reason and we do not stop teaching once we are outside of the classroom. Your tuition is paying our salary so use us to help you succeed.

Tests: Before the Test and Anxiety

I cannot count the number of times I have heard the phrase "I'm not a good test taker." I strongly believe that anyone can be good at taking tests but there are those that struggle with their test grades. I do not believe that poor test scores are a result of poor test taking skills. I feel that poor test scores and test anxiety are the result of three primary factors: Not studying enough or not studying the correct information, trying to cram in the classroom right before the test, and your activities on all the other days you're in that class.

First, study for the examination. Learning and improving study habits will play a crucial role in improving poor test scores. Test anxiety for many students comes from not being fully prepared and the more prepared you are, the less anxiety you will have. You will still have some sense of urgency but knowing the material takes much of that stress away.

Second, relax as much as possible right before the test. Something I see at every single in-class exam troubles me. I walk in the room and several students are frantically thumbing through their notes, study guides, or flashcards. I always say the same thing to them: Stop, put your notes away because if you do not know it now, you are not going to. While that may sound negative, I make another point to follow up the first one. I tell them that all they are doing is stressing themselves out and that leads to second-guessing and anxiety. I always suggest that they do one of two things. I tell them to just come in, find a place they are comfortable, set up anything they need to, and then just sit. Alternatively, I advise that they stay outside of the classroom until the last minute. By doing so, they stay out of an environment where others are stressed, allow themselves some fresh air, and can just walk in and take the test. I always give this advice to students who are planning to take the LSAT as well.

Rebekah (the recent graduate) disagreed about looking over notes prior to the exam but agreed with me in relation to the anxiety. She said: "It is definitely not the most efficient habit to have to look at your notes right before a test because if you don't know the information then you won't know it for the test. However, I do have a habit of doing a once over glance of all of my notes before an exam (kind of like a checklist thing) because there have been questions on tests that I would not have known the exact answer. I am grateful that I double-checked that answer again before starting the test. So, it can work as a sort of checklist/once over glance but not as a last minute cramming session that will heighten your anxiety." This seems like good advice if you can approach it in the way she suggests.

Third, so much of test taking success comes from all the times you are in class. You should examine or reexamine what you do in class and how you do it. Sitting in the front of the class increases both participation and attentiveness. Coming to class having read and memorized the material, as well as effective note taking, can make a world of difference. Lastly, asking questions of the professor in class and during their office hours is crucial.

On a final note regarding test taking and nervousness, it will be incredibly important for you to eat and sleep before the test. Food equals energy so eat a healthy breakfast or lunch before the test. Just work hard not to weigh yourself down with heavy foods, especially at lunch before an afternoon exam. It may bog you down a bit and you want to be full of as much energy as possible. You also want to get a good night's sleep before the test and get out of bed well ahead of your test time since it takes a bit for the brain to wake up.

Tests: Taking the Test

A few other pieces of advice are warranted in relation to test taking. When taking the test, make sure you answer all of the questions and all parts of each question and do so in a way that answers exactly what the question asks. It sounds like silly advice but so many students lose points because they leave short-answer questions blank, do not answer all the parts of a question or just do not answer what was asked. Remember that we can only grade based on what you wrote and we cannot know what you were thinking when you wrote it. So, when answering, make sure you are writing down exactly what you are thinking. Mark up the test if necessary so you are absolutely clear about how many parts to each question there are. Give us as professors the chance to give you at least partial credit.

Leave the questions you do not know the answer to and come back later to them. Look at other parts of the test for help with questions you do not know the answer to. You never know if your memory will be sparked by another question.

If your professor gives you an option between multiple choice and short-answer or short essay questions, you will always want to take the short-answer or essay option. Many students think that multiple-choice tests are easier and while that may be true in high school, it is not true in college. Professors can be very sneaky with multiple-choice questions and we can make them very difficult. Remember, with multiple-choice questions, you are choosing the *best* answer and that implies that more than one answer can be correct. That makes it very difficult.

When you do take multiple-choice tests, use the process of elimination rather than working to immediately identify the right answer. Many students read the answers very quickly to pick out the correct one and that can lead to mistakes. By going through and eliminating incorrect choices, you will slow down and it will force you to read all the options.

When taking a short-answer examination, do not rewrite the question in the answer. So many students do this and it is unnecessary and wastes a great deal of time and hand strength. We wrote the question and don't need to be reminded of what it was in your answer. Abbreviate as much as allowed. If you are not required to write in proper English, do not.

Time management is another major consideration when taking tests. Read the directions, read all of the questions, take note of how much each question is worth and then plan your attack. Many students answer the easy ones first while others move straight through. Many students make marks or notations near question numbers indicating that the question was one they did not automatically know the answer to. I feel this is a good technique because it identifies a question you will need to go back for. If you adopt the strategies from the paragraph above or find one of your own that works for you, you should have plenty of time. Professors work hard to make the tests both fair and able to be completed in the time allotted.

There are scores of books and websites that speak to test taking techniques and I absolutely suggest that you read some of those sources. I do not have all the answers but the suggestions I am giving here work.

Other techniques work as well so the more guidance you can get the better.

Tests: After the Test

Remember, we can only grade what you wrote and how close that is to the right answer. We cannot and will not grade you based on what we thought you meant by your answer. If you get your exam back and are unhappy (regardless of whether your grade was high or low) do not go to your professor and ask for a higher grade because you did not make your answer clear.

On the other hand, if you are sure you gave the right answer, partially or wholly, and you can show proof, then it is appropriate to ask the professor to review that particular question. Just assure that you do so in a respectful manner. Professors are human and we make mistakes. It happens but we will own up to them and change your grade.

Papers

Big research papers can be daunting to write. Many first year students come to college never having written anything over five or seven pages long. Ten or more page papers in college are the norm, not the exception. Not having written papers this long, like any other unknown, makes students nervous about their ability to complete them. This section will give advice that will help you succeed at efficiently writing papers, even if you do not believe you are a solid writer. I will address the process of writing a paper and my hope is that you can become a more efficient writer. Learning how to become a better and more efficient writer are lifelong skills that will be more beneficial than you can imagine.

Don't Cut Corners

Throughout my entire teaching career, students consistently add 'fluff' to their papers or modify the format to make the minimum page limit. As a general rule, we spot that in an instant and by adding fluff, you are clearly notifying us that you are cutting corners. In other words, we are very aware when you decrease the margins, increase your font size or increase the spacing between lines. Do not add extra double spaces between paragraphs since the indentation is enough for us to know you are changing topics. Do not increase the pitch (distance between letters). Because of these experiences happening more often than we would like, many professors, myself included, have moved to a word count because that eliminates the impact of formatting modifications. Simply put, avoid cutting corners because we will most certainly notice.

Understand What is Being Asked of You

Many students approach me with questions about papers that I and other professors assign to them because they are not sure what that professor is looking for. Either the syllabus or assignment handout was vague or the verbal instructions by the professor were unclear. I always give the same advice and that is to go speak with the professor. It makes no logical sense to think that you know what the professor wants in a paper unless they specifically tell you. The smart thing would be to meet with the professor and ask for clarification with clear, pointed questions. If you ever ask yourself whether what you are writing is what the professor wants, immediately stop and go meet with the professor. We will not mind and we will not take offense, I promise.

Start Early

Each month of every single semester is busier than the preceding month. You are going to be *so much* busier in November than you were in August or September. With this in mind, why wouldn't you write that ten-page paper in the beginning of the semester when you have much more time compared to when you have finals approaching and other papers coming due? It is sometimes difficult to feel the sense of urgency to write your papers early but once you do it the first time, you will never go back to waiting again. While everyone else is stressed out and staying up all night, your paper will be done, edited, proofed and ready to submit.

In graduate school, I put the due dates for my big papers one week before they were actually due. I would work all semester but would always, without fail,

131

make sure those papers were ready to hand in that full week early. It is so much easier to go into the end of the semester with one big paper off your plate but it takes perseverance and commitment to follow through with this.

Just be careful not to write most of your paper early and then leave it for weeks. Letting it sit for a short amount of time is fine as long as you are thinking, brainstorming or organizing the paper. I just do not want you to forget about the paper or procrastinate, and then come back to it right when it's due. I had one student that wrote a fantastic paper for the first seven out of ten pages. The last three, however, were fraught with proofing and spelling errors. When I asked about this, he simply said he had finished those last three pages right before the class. Start early and give yourself the chance to finish early. This technique also allows you to submit drafts to your professor, which can increase your grade more than you could imagine.

I am fully aware that many students wait until the last minute to write papers, both larger term papers and smaller ones. I cannot stop you from doing this. If the sense of urgency isn't there and you have high levels of procrastination, then you will find yourself stuck writing that big paper right before it's due and pulling an all-nighter. The only thing I can say here is that it is *highly* likely that your paper will not get the grade you want. Since term papers are usually a good percentage of your final grade, the final grade in the class will suffer.

Organization

When I was completing my dissertation, my brother (also a Ph.D.) gave me some rather simplistic advice about writing and organization. He told me to, "Tell them what you're going to write about. Write about it. Tell them what you wrote." You may think that this just means that you need to have an introduction to the paper, the body and a conclusion, and while that is true, it goes a bit deeper. He told me to follow this formula throughout the entire paper, including each section and even each paragraph (topic sentence, body, concluding sentence and transition). This may feel like fluff to you or you may think that it makes your paper boring and repetitive. However, a well-organized paper that leads the reader easily down the path makes all the difference. We read so many papers that it is actually a relief to dig into a paper that is clear and well organized. It makes us happy! Let me put it this way: A well-organized paper that lacks some content will probably receive a better grade than one that is disorganized. With the disorganized paper, it is difficult for us to understand what points you are trying to make. In other words, papers have two goals that you need to keep in mind. Content is obviously crucial but papers need to be well written and organized at the same time. Your grade will come from some balance of the two.

The Absolute Best Way to Write a Paper

Students write papers using very different techniques. Some students do their research and put that research directly into the paper. Some take notes or make index cards and then transfer those notes to

133

the paper. Some just sit down and write (please do not do this).

I want to tell you about the absolute best way to write a research paper. This may be a bit of an exaggeration but if you start and perfect this technique, you will write well-organized papers in an extremely efficient fashion. You will also not worry as much about making the page or word limit since you are working to organize content as you are doing your research. If done correctly, the page count will fall into place. Trust me on this one. Below is my advice for writing a paper, especially a longer term paper.

> **Make an Outline.** Make an outline in a Word document and include everything you think you need to address in the order you think would be most organized. You do not want to have a handwritten outline because that will force you to record the same information twice; once handwritten and once into the outline or paper. Use a normal Roman numeral outlining system making sure that you start with an introduction and end with a conclusion. Be sure to look at the syllabus or handout that the professor gives you and use that to guide your outline. Listen to what the professor has to say when they are going over the paper in class.

With the body of the outline, start with the main headings. These should be all the larger categories you feel need to be included. You can always change this as you research and the more you research, the more the outline will change. Do not worry about this. Add subheadings as needed. The benefit is that you have a template to start with. When you write

134

in these main headings, look to see if they make sense organizationally. Do they logically flow from one to the next? If based on chronological events, make sure your outline works chronologically as well. Organization and flow are crucial to writing a solid paper.

After you start researching, you will have an outline with headings that flow together and flow logically. Remember, you are telling a story about your topic and it needs to make sense. For example, if you were writing a paper about the presidency, you would not talk about the current state of the presidency without first talking about presidential history, right? If you are at all unsure about your outline or even if you think it is perfect, bring it to the professor for their feedback. Make sure you either take great notes in that meeting or bring your laptop so you can modify the outline as you are talking about it. I even allow students to record our conversations on their phone so they can go back and review it later. For only thirty minutes of your time, why wouldn't you?

➢ **Read Your First Source and Take Notes Directly into your Outline.** Now, read your first source. As you encounter *any* information you feel should be in your paper, type this information into your outline under the specific heading or subheading that it belongs in. Then cite the work right where you put it in whichever citing system you are using (i.e. APA). Now go back to the source you are reading and as you come across the next piece of information do the same thing. Rinse and repeat until you have finished reading that single source. You should find that you have used that source in several distinct areas in your paper. Now, start a reference page and write in the correct reference. Using a website for this can help you be correct, consistent and complete with your references.

➢ **Read the Rest of Your Sources and Take Notes Directly into your Outline.** Follow this exact same pattern for each source you read. Whether it be a book, website or academic journal, take notes right into the outline as you go, cite in the outline as you go and then put the entire citation into your reference page. If you have to add or delete headings or subheadings as you go, feel free to do so. If you do, make sure you keep a sharp eye on the outline to assure that it is still organized in the way you need it to be so it flows smoothly from topic to topic.

If you follow this simple pattern, you will see several significant benefits. Your paper will be properly organized because you paid attention to it from the start. You will also have taken all your notes and they should all be in their relevant sections. You have written them directly into what will be your paper rather than writing them on cards or in your notebook and then transferring them. In other words, you have read and taken notes in one-step rather than two steps. Why take three hours per source rather than two hours? It does not make sense not to do this!

By writing your paper this way, you only needed to look at your sources one time and you only took notes on them one time. Fourth, you are able to cite in the body of your paper without going back to look at the sources themselves because you wrote the cite in your outline next to the notes that you took from it. Lastly, since you completed your reference page at the same time you did your research, it is done!

Working through your paper this way also makes it so much easier to actually write the paper. When your outline is done, all you need to do is to make sentences and paragraphs within each major section and subsections. You have already written the paper in outline form so now all you have to do is clean it up, synthesize the information, and write more formally. Just look at all the notes you have written from all your different sources and put them together to make one cohesive section. Then do the same for all the sections in the paper. Just make sure you are making sense of your notes rather than just putting them in the paper in a particular order. You want to make sure that you are writing your paper instead of your sources.

This system is incredibly efficient. By practicing and honing this process, you will save countless hours writing papers. I have been using this technique in my academic writing for my entire career and it has saved me more time than I could tell you.

Submit Drafts

I want to make a single logical statement that clearly exemplifies why you should submit paper drafts especially in classes you are struggling in. If you submit a draft, the professor will tell you everything that is wrong with it. If you fix what the professor tells you to fix, how can you not get a higher grade? The answer is that you will always get a higher grade if you submit drafts. Always. The only time that I have not given a higher grade to someone who submitted a draft was when he or she did not fix a single thing that I suggested. Other than that, everyone gets a higher grade.

So, the question you are likely asking is this: What does a draft actually entail? The simple answer is that a draft is the first copy of your entire paper. This draft needs to be spellchecked and fully proofread like a final draft, it should have all your citations in the body of the paper and it should have a reference page. It is fine if the paper is not where you want it to be. As professors, we know you are coming to us for guidance so that you can write a better paper.

While few professors might accept only full drafts, the majority of us will accept smaller sections of your paper. So, if you finish a section or even just your introduction, ask if you can send it. You can even send a working outline. The reason that we will be receptive is that it is easier and much quicker to review a small part of your paper instead of the whole thing. In addition, we know that if you are submitting a draft, you have worked hard and early, and want to do well. Submit drafts and I guarantee that your paper grades will increase.

Asking for Extensions

As a general rule, it does not work to your benefit to ask for an extension to a big paper. You are simply telling the professor that while you have had all semester to work on it, you chose not to and instead waited until the last minute. This may sound very harsh, but if you have an illness or other major problem right before your paper is due and ask for an extension, you are still telling the professor that you chose not to work on the paper over the course of the entire semester.

138

Also, my experience shows that asking for an extension may not necessarily lead to a better grade. If you have the paper almost done and can *make it better* with that extra time (even with a late penalty) then go for it. On the other hand, if you have waited until the last minute to do the bulk of the work, your logic is flawed if you believe you will suddenly gain a burst of writing energy and submit a solid product. The fact that you are asking for an extension still shows you have struggled with procrastination, time management, or both. As I said before, work early and work often. It pays off.

Academic Sources and Research

Undoubtedly, you have used the Internet for academic research. You may even have become fairly adept at it. What you may not realize is that the Internet (i.e. Google) is a terrible place to start your research. Anyone can put up a web page and say whatever they want on it. Any information found is both unreliable and not acceptable for most college level papers, especially courses in the social sciences (psychology, sociology, etc.). Below you will find a few quick rules on choosing and using academic sources.

➤ **Do not use Wikipedia, ever.**

➤ **If a web page states that they got their information from a more reliable academic source, you should go to that reliable academic source.**

➤ **Reliable academic sources for papers include government websites, academic journals and academic books. Google Scholar can also yield solid academic sources.**

➤ **If there are advertisements on the page, it is likely not acceptable.**

➤ **Sites that end in .com are generally not acceptable.**

If your source does fall under one of these last four of these categories, it would be smart to show the link to your professor and ask if it is appropriate before you submit your paper. Each major may have their own rule for what is appropriate but it is better to err on the side of using academic sources than it is non-academic ones. It is also better to ask first than be penalized later.

In relation to citing sources in your paper, you always want to over-cite to avoid charges of plagiarism. It is better to be safe than sorry. The general rule is that if the information was not common knowledge and did not come from your own mind, you must cite it. Also, if you are using a sentence right out of one of your sources, you must put the phrase in quotation marks indicating you are copying this verbatim. Lastly, you never want to have only one source in a single paragraph. You want to have at least two or more.

If you only use one source, that tells the professor that you are regurgitating information from each source individually. That equates to writing short book reports and that is not what college is all about. You need to be able to make sense of the research and reiterating what one author said then moving to another should be avoided at all cost.

Classroom Etiquette

Disrespect takes many forms in a classroom and it is not just verbal. You need to act like an adult. Acting without regard for others is disrespectful and if you do one of the items on the list below, you will likely hear about it, either in front of the class or in your professor's office.

> ➤ **Keep your cell phone on silent and in your bag.** We will make sure you get out of class on time. Texting in class is utterly disrespectful and will not be tolerated. By the way, when you put both of your hands under your desk and continually look down and up, we know you are texting – we are not stupid. In my class, I mark you absent if I catch you texting and that lowers your grade substantially. If your phone rings in my class, I will answer it for you. If you have an emergency that requires you to be near your phone, put it on vibrate, sit near the door, and tell the professor you may need to walk out to answer your phone. They will appreciate that. As a side note, when high school seniors sit in on one of my classes and they get on their phone, I immediately call them out. If you visit a college and sit in on a class, do not think the professor will not let you know that being on your phone is unacceptable.

> ➤ **Be on time.** It is not that difficult and when you are late, it disrupts the entire class. If you are more than twenty minutes late, just do not go and take the absence.

➢ **You should not eat in class but if you have to do not eat stinky or loud food.** I do not need to tell you why.

➢ **Do not use profanity.** Sometimes the professor will (usually by accident) but that does not give you permission.

➢ **Feel free to question others' positions but only if you have the facts.** Your opinion may not be supported by fact and you will just embarrass yourself. College is all about learning that not everything is black and white and that there are views different from yours that may be supported by evidence. Learn to tell the difference and that skill will follow you through life.

➢ **Do not attack another student or the professor personally because they disagree with you.** That is the quickest way to be thrown out of class. Feel free to question the professor (supported by facts) but do not disrespect them. We really do love engaging in intellectual discussion but you should not disagree solely because of your past experience or what you heard somewhere.

➢ **Any disrespect toward the professor will not be tolerated.** Whether you meant it or not, disrespect toward a professor is inappropriate and will result in negative consequences, and those consequences will vary by professor.

Getting into Closed Classes

This is a big one and if you do it right, it is a technique that will work magic for you. I have spoken about this in past chapters but it deserves reiteration. Upper class students will register first and if you are registering for classes after the seniors, juniors and sophomores, it is likely that courses you would like to take will be closed because they are at maximum capacity. If this is the case, you will not be able to register for them. If you want to find out if a class you want is likely to fill up, look at the class schedule pages from the previous semesters. If they are full or close to full, they will likely fill before you get a chance to register.

What you need to do is stop by and see the professor (preferred method) or email them. Tell them you really want to take the class and that the content looks very exciting. Tell them that you think the class is going to fill before you get a chance to register and that you would like to be on the wait list, even before registration starts. Students inevitably drop the class or leave school over the break and if you are first on the wait list, it almost guarantees your entry into the class.

Most colleges have students register online on a specific day and time each semester. As you move forward in your college career, you can avoid needing to get into closed classes by registering the minute your time to register opens up. You can do it from the comfort of your dorm room but you may want to get off campus at registration time. Remember, all of the other students in your year are trying to register simultaneously and the college network may slow down quite a bit. You can avoid dealing with a slow college network by getting off campus when you register. As an FYI, the same holds true for the end of the semester when big papers and finals are due. At those times, the college's network really slows down.

Becoming a Better Writer

Not everyone is a great writer and in fact, very few are – professors included. That being said, writing is a skill that you will use every day at work and you need to be able to write well. The time to work on your writing is now. Researching early and efficiently, and submitting drafts are all crucial but writing is a skill that needs continual honing. We are happy to help. We are not happy, however, when you get the same advice about your writing over and over and refuse to fix or address it. If we give you advice about how to improve aspects of your writing, you need to take advantage so you can improve.

Conclusion

The goal of this chapter was to give you advice that will help you succeed in your classes. More specifically, I want you to gain good habits early on so you can be successful at testing, writing papers and navigating college. As I have said several times before, most of these skills and techniques addressed above can be used in high school letting you get started before you even head off to college.

The advice I have given in this chapter is by no means complete, there are many sources both online, and in print that will help. What makes this advice important is that it is coming from a seasoned professor's point of view. In other words, if you employ these techniques, professors will notice and your grades will likely rise. You are making an effort to improve and that is what we really care about, regardless of where you started.

In the next chapter, the focus will be on efficiency *outside* the classroom because it is just as important. Your time is valuable and so many students do not think about utilizing the time outside of academics as wisely as they should. The chapter will focus on things you can do that will save you a great deal of time when not in class.

Being an Effective & Efficient Student - Administrative Tasks

Introduction

You do not have all the time in the world so use it wisely. Knowing how to read and study, and excel at tests and papers is only half the battle. You also need to be efficient and effective at the administrative tasks that will make college (and life) much easier for you. You need to know the best way to set up your schedule and work toward graduation as quickly as you can. You also need to learn how to save time with your daily tasks.

As an example, students will bring their laptops to my office and then access their email. To do that, they open their browser, type in the college's main email address, and navigate three pages to get to their email. Why not put a direct link on your bookmark toolbar? It does not make sense not to. Why spend three minutes completing a task you do often when you can spend five to ten minutes setting up a system that allows you to do the same task in one minute or less? Saving a few seconds or minutes may not seem like a lot but when you do the task over and over, you will save more time than you know.

In this chapter, I will give you guidance with the tasks like the one above but I will not walk you through any specific steps. That is your job. Learning for yourself will help you and it will allow you to help others. This is what college is all about. College helps you become independent and confident. I strongly believe it is invaluable to give advice that will support your academics and save you hours. That being said, giving you the answers or direct steps for a task will be a disservice to you now and once you get out. So, I will walk you to the front steps but you will need to learn how to walk through the door.

The other important message you should take away from this chapter is that you can start doing many of these now while you are still in high school. Knowing how to do these tasks can help ease your transition in a significant way. The fewer changes that you go through when you get to college, the easier the transition will be. Moreover, the advice about health and roommates gives you an idea of what to expect so you can make changes in preparation for college. So, start using the skills I give you in this chapter because being an effective and efficient student now will make you so much more effective once you get to college.

Academic Progress Toward Graduation

Succeeding in academics is more than just getting good grades. You need to think about your academic progress as well. By this, I mean that you have to think about how to get into courses, how to manage your schedule so it works for you and how to balance out the difficult courses with the less difficult ones. This section focuses on administrative skills that will help you get toward graduation sooner and with less stress.

Template for Each Semester

During every semester, you should take classes that are required to graduate. Most schools require you to complete a major, a minor and general education requirements (i.e. math, science, language, English). They want you to be very knowledgeable in your major but also want you to be well rounded so you do not become an astrophysicist who only knows about astrophysics.

When thinking about a plan for the upcoming semester, each course should fit one of these requirements. I like to suggest that once a student knows what they want to major in, they should take two courses in that major, one course in their minor, and one or two general education requirements. Sometimes, one course may count for two requirements. For example, an introduction to psychology class might count for the psychology major and a general education requirement. You should ask your advisor about this and if you can double count requirements, you should.

Many students want to take all their general education requirements as first years or sophomores so they can focus on their major as juniors and seniors. While there is benefit in that scheme, it will do you more harm than good. Waiting until your sophomore or junior year to start your major assumes that all the courses you will need will be offered exactly when you need them. That is not something you want to bet your graduation on. Also, balancing an easy general education course with harder upper level courses makes more sense in the end. When you are taking the major capstone class in your senior year, having an easier class in your schedule will make a world of difference. If you maintain this balance throughout your college career, it puts a sense of regularity into your schedule. Over the course of multiple semesters, this will help.

Rebekah, a 2017 graduate said: "I completely agree with scheduling in a balanced way when planning your course load. I have had friends make a plan where they get requirements out of the way in the first two years, but then they have crappy junior and senior years because they are bogged down with heavy course loads. Also, in my experience, it is nice to have that chill, kinda carefree class. It lets your academic brain relax a little and enjoy the learning of some new material."

Now, if you are like most incoming first years and do not know exactly what you want to major in, it is ok. Personally, I do not feel that a college freshman should choose what they want to do with their life when they are 18 years old. College is a time for figuring that out. If you have already figured it out, then start taking courses in your major right away. If not, take courses that fit general education requirements but that also are in the discipline that you are thinking of majoring in. By doing so, you have fulfilled a general

150

education requirement even if you do not choose that major. If you do choose the major, you have now filled one its requirements. It is a win-win situation and this scheme gives you time to look around at different majors. By the middle of your sophomore year, however, you should be ready to choose a major and move forth with those classes.

Science, Math and A Foreign Language – Take Them Now!

Many students do not like or have a phobia about math, science and language classes. I understand this but strongly encourage you to get these requirements out of the way during your first year. They may not make you happy but you will definitely be happy when they are done. You will never be as close to science, math, and languages as you are right now so waiting for a few years after high school is a mistake. You will retain a good deal of information from your high school classes but over time, you lose some of it. This leads students to avoid those classes until the very last minute and that can only hurt you. Take them early if only to get them out of the way. As a side note, if you take a language early, it might help you if you choose to study abroad, which you absolutely should.

Your Weekly Schedule

Only you know what is best for you. There are times when you are very effective at studying and when your brain is at its most active. There are times when the opposite is true. For me, I get six hours of work done in three hours in the morning but I only get three hours of work done in six hours in the afternoon. As a result, I get up early, schedule my classes mostly in the morning when possible and leave my afternoons more open knowing that I will struggle to get work done. After your first semester, you will hopefully be able to schedule your classes so you do not have to take the dreaded 8:00am class. This is not a guarantee but with the information in this book, you will be better positioned to schedule classes around what works for you. There are a few pieces of advice that I can give here in relation to setting up your weekly schedule.

First, try to make your schedule so you wake up at the same time every day. While afternoon classes enable you to sleep until noon or one that is not the way to go. Mid or late morning classes every day will help get your body into a solid routine. Second, work hard to have no more than three classes in one day. Your mind will get tired. I realize that you went to high school for seven hours a day but college is not the same. Also, you will regret having so much work due every week on the same day.

Third, work to schedule no more than two classes in a row. Having three classes in a row is a very bad idea. Not only is it difficult to stay afloat with the work but having your mind go from Spanish to Math to Biology all in a few hours is very difficult. Your third class will suffer in relation to both your attention and your work quality. Also, this will probably keep you from having lunch.

Having three classes in a row also leads to you being tired and less responsive in class. You might even fall asleep and you want to avoid that at all cost. Back in the old days, I used to throw erasers at students who fell asleep but since violence in the classroom is rightfully frowned upon, I now whisper in the student's ear to wake up. Once that happens, they never fall asleep in my class again because it is just embarrassing.

Lastly, spreading out your classes over the course of the week is better than finishing them over two or three days. If you have no classes two days of the week, your schedule will be off kilter and it may inhibit your work ethic. Later in your college career, if you believe it is a good idea for you, then I am all for it but for your first year, it would be smart to avoid this pattern.

Respect in Your Communications with Faculty

When a student is disrespectful to me, I always have the same response. I email them and write: "Please come to my office so we can discuss the way you choose to communicate with faculty." This is an email that no student wants to get from me. I do not yell or berate but I am very clear about how I simply will not tolerate disrespect. Once I have expressed myself and the student apologizes, I move on with no hard feelings. Just know that this conversation is not very fun for the student. As faculty, we have more experience in school than any undergraduate student does. We have advanced degrees and it is imperative that you behave in a way that is respectful. Even if you are on a first name basis with a professor (it is not wholly unheard of), you still must be respectful of boundaries.

Disrespect need not be intentional and in fact, some students will say or do something disrespectful and not even know it. This could be in person or via email or voicemail. Many years ago, I had my first year seminar students over to my house for dinner. One student expressed to me "your wife is hot." His disrespect was not intentional but it was. When writing an email, be more formal than you think you need to be. Include using proper salutations and avoid using text speak at all cost. Paul Corrigan and Cameron Hunt McNabb wrote a great short piece that focuses on writing emails to faculty. (https://www.insidehighered.com/views/2015/04/1 6/advice-students-so-they-dont-sound-silly-emails-essay). Just be sensitive to the level of respect you give to faculty, staff and other students in and out of class.

Go to Class

I know I spoke of this before but it deserves another mention. You should go to every class because you are in college and this is why you are here. You want to avoid unnecessary and unexcused absences. They are the easiest way to have your grade lowered substantially, even if you do well in the other areas. While some professors do not take attendance, many do and there will likely be a section in the syllabus about that professor's absence policy. You want to note that each professor can and probably will have very different policies when it comes to attendance. Some will copy and paste out of the student handbook and others will modify. In my classes, I allow three excused or unexcused absences and I do not differentiate between them.

With this in mind, you will need to be very careful about if or when you decide to skip classes. I suggest that you read and fully understand the policy at the beginning of the semester. If a professor does allow a certain number of absences without impacting your grade, work hard not to use them. Also, work extra hard *not* to use them in the beginning of the semester. The grades of students who skip early on in the semester often get negatively impacted because they get sick later on, after they have used up all their absences. The advice is to do not miss a class unless you really need to. However, if you are going to skip, wait until after fall break so early absences do not come back to haunt you. In any case, you need to be absolutely clear as to what the absence policy is in each and every class before making any decisions to skip or sleep in.

Student Success Center

Colleges want you to come and be a student there. Once you are there, they want you to stay. Retention, the percentage of students who come back between their first and second year, is a benchmark to see how well a college is doing at keeping their students. Because they want you to stay and succeed, they have a multitude of resources that students can take advantage of. You may think that you know best, but there are so many college employees whose job it is to help you succeed. While faculty are part of this group, the employees who can help you the most with being an effective and efficient student are in the college's student success or learning center. These centers go by many different names but all colleges have them. The people that work in these centers have the skills and experience to give you advice that is specific to you and your learning style. This is what they do all day every day. It is their job, so they have seen it all. They will not come to you, however, so you need to go to them and let them help you. Trust me on this one. They have likely helped thousands of students before you who have had the same problems as you do.

When asked, a senior said to me, "This is absolutely 100% true. Use your resources. I would also mention that Career Development Centers can assist with your student success. Personally, that resource yielded the best results for me and helped me succeed in areas I would not have imagined. The student learning centers are super beneficial too. You should use them now because that is what they are there for, and students have easy access to them. Out of school, you would need to pay someone in order to receive their help for things like this. It's free and readily available, so you really should use them."

Efficiency and Your Computer

You spend a great deal of time on your electronic devices. You surf the web, check your email and watch videos. You also complete much of your schoolwork on your computer. While rumor has it that some students actually write papers on their cell phones (which I just cannot fathom), most still write them on their laptop or desktop.

With this in mind, I give some advice that will allow you to be much more efficient with your computer. I want you to be able to access web pages and files quickly. I also do not want you to lose papers because your computer crashes. Sorry to say, but that excuse does not work anymore. In this section, you will find important advice that can save you a great deal of time and frustration when using your computer.

The Bookmark Toolbar

Every Internet browser has a bookmarks toolbar. This toolbar allows you to go to a specific website with one click rather than three or four clicks, or by having to type the URL into the browser directly. It may sound silly but any small move you can make that will save you time should absolutely be utilized. Browsers like Chrome, Firefox and Safari all differ but a quick Google search can tell you how to use the bookmark toolbar. You may find that your toolbar fills up quickly so abbreviating web page names allows room for more bookmarks. For instance, if you bookmark your email page, it might show up as 'Yahoo! Mail.' You can change this to 'YM' or another abbreviation that you will recognize.

The idea here is that you can spend a few minutes setting up a system that makes it easier and faster for you to do your regular tasks. Saving five seconds does not seem like much but if you add up all that saved time over the period of an entire semester, it can be quite substantial. As a busy college professor, I have to make efforts to shave any wasted time off my schedule. It makes an amazing difference and allows me to be efficient with my time. The same technique will work for you.

Your Home Page

During the academic school year, my home page is my college email inbox. I check my email often and keep it on my screen most of the time when I am working. I always have multiple tabs open so I can keep my email open on one tab. This way, I never have to navigate back to it if I go surfing elsewhere. I also have my computer set up so my browser starts when my computer starts up without me having to click on anything. You can also have more than one tab open up when your browser starts. I do think it would be smart for your college email to open upon startup. I realize that some students may not check their college email as often but you should (see next section). While you can choose to have whatever website you visit most often as your home page, I would strongly recommend that it *not* be a social media website such as Facebook or YouTube. These sites can draw you in and end up taking a great deal of your time before you even start the homework you need to do.

Use Your College Email

Every college will assign you a college email address and you should absolutely use that as your primary email address. Most email companies make it quite simple to import all your past email and contacts and if you struggle, the college IT department will always help you. The only place that faculty will contact you is through your college email address. Also, student handbooks at many colleges state that you must check your college email every twenty-four hours. If we, as faculty, contact you via your college email about a deadline and you do not respond because you did not check it, you will likely get little sympathy. Moreover, if you email from a private email account and do not identify yourself as one of our students, we might be less likely to even open the email for fear of downloading a virus.

More and more colleges are offering an email address for life. So, if you graduate from that college or university, you will be able to keep that email address after you leave. It is great for colleges because they can reach out to you with college news or to keep track of you as one of their graduates. This is also smart because college email systems have fairly strong spam filters and reducing your spam helps you reduce wasted time.

More and more colleges are also using Google Apps for Education. In short, this means that Google is hosting the college's email and that while you will have an .edu email address from your school; it is really just Gmail without the ads. As of 2015, there were over 70 million users (Lardinois, 2017) and predictions have that number doubling by 2020 (Boost eLearning, 2015). This means that more and more colleges will by using Gmail (with their own .edu address) as time passes so learning how to use and be efficient at Gmail will be important.

If you do choose to keep your current email address in addition to your college email address, I do have a suggestion. If your college utilizes Gmail for their mail server, I would suggest using two different browsers; one for your personal email address and one for your college email address. I suggest this because Google and browsers get a bit cranky when you want to be logged in to several Gmail accounts at the same time. If your college and personal email accounts are not both from Gmail, then place both on your bookmark toolbar, so you can have quick and easy access to them.

One last suggestion about using the college email. In most email programs, you can apply labels to emails to categorize them and Gmail is included. I never delete emails. Instead, I create labels, place the correct label with the email and then archive it. I have never run out of space and if organized correctly, I can access every single email I have received or sent over the past decade. I have labels for each class I teach, my department, committees, and one for general college-related email. It would be worth researching how to make and manage labels in Gmail or whatever email program your college employs. Lastly, a student recently made a great suggestion to me to tell you. She said that you should always archive emails from professors under a separate label. Smart.

Sign up for a Free Cloud Based Storage Service

Gone are the days where "my computer crashed" was a good excuse for not turning in your work. Make no mistake, computers still crash and data is lost but there is a very simple and effective way to avoid it. You should sign up for a free cloud-based storage service such as Dropbox or Google Backup and Sync. They are simple and quick to set up, even for those who are not technologically savvy. Once it is done, all your papers and class work will be saved in the cloud and you can access them from any device that is connected to the Internet.

It works like this. First, you work through the set up process, which prompts you to pick which folders you want saved in the cloud. Once you make those choices, then every time you save a file on your computer or laptop, it also automatically saves it to your cloud server if you have an Internet connection. If you are not connected to the Internet at that time, it will automatically save to the cloud when it your connection returns. You also do not have to save it twice or save it in more than one place (i.e. a flash drive). Moreover, you will be able to access the file on computers, tablets and smartphones, and you will likely never run out of space while you are in college. I have twenty years of teaching materials saved in the cloud and have never run out of space. Just do not save your photographs or music in the cloud because if you do, you might just run out of space. Google Photos works great for saving your pictures.

Alternatively, many use Google Drive. If your college uses Gmail, you automatically have Google Drive and if they do not, just start a Gmail account and you will have automatic access. Students seem to love Google Drive because it is very easy to use. When working in groups, multiple students can edit at the same time and changes can be seen in real time. As an FYI, Google Drive does experience some minor formatting problems if you have to bring the document back to your word processor so make sure you proof your work when you submit Word files. Work to research which method is the best for you but whatever you do, have an efficient system in place to assure you do not lose your work.

161

The Dreaded Desktop: Setting up an Efficient File System

I cannot describe how many times students come into my office with their computers and have a hundred or more files on their desktop, many of which are school related. This is problematic for several reasons.

> ➢ **It is difficult to find a needle in a haystack.**

> ➢ **It is disorganized and incredibly inefficient.** Having so many files or folders on your desktop may increase the time it takes to find a file and it may actually increase anxiety. Think about a dresser in your bedroom where you do not organize your clothes and instead, every drawer holds shirts, pants, socks, etc. This doesn't make much sense because it will be difficult, time consuming and frustrating for you to find that one shirt or pair of pants. So why do that same thing on your computer? Why take a minute to find something that could take you five seconds to find?

> ➢ **Your desktop cannot be backed up to many cloud-based storage services**. As I suggested above, you absolutely must have a backup mechanism in place in college.

I would strongly suggest that you do not save individual files and assignments on your desktop. Instead, put them in their relevant folders and allow them to be backed up in the cloud. On my desktop, I have my list of programs that I use most often as well as a few folders and my 'to do' list. I do download files from the web onto my desktop for efficiency of finding the file with one click but I either delete it when done or immediately put it in its relevant folder. Keeping a nice clean desktop can be less problematic and stressful than one with rows and rows of files, folders and applications.

Let me make a suggestion here. You should consider making separate folders for each of your courses as well as separate sub-folders in each class for term paper materials, administrative materials and normal course materials. Remember that your computer (Windows or Mac) organizes files and folders first by numbers and then alphabetically. What this means is that file and folder names with numbers will be listed first and then alphabetically after that. Any folders or files that you want to have on top of the list should always start with a number. Also, make sure to use the same pattern in each folder because it makes it easier to find what you need. For example, every folder I have for each class is organized the same way with the first four folders being administrative in nature and the remaining folders having course content. Below you will see a screenshot of one of my course folders (this folder is from a Mac but Windows Explorer organizes folders in exactly the same fashion). Notice that I have 0-1 in front of the first folder name. This will always come up first and I move down from there (0-2, 0-3 etc.). Class content always starts with a 1. This system works very well for me but how you choose to organize is up to you. Just make sure you set it up so you are able to find and open any file from any class in just a few clicks.

Know Your College's Website and Learning Management System

Know your college's website and where to find what you need. Whether it be access to the library, research databases or course schedules, being able to navigate and know where to go is important. There will be specific college websites that may not warrant putting on the bookmark toolbar but you still want to be able to get to them quickly. You will save time and frustration. Your knowledge of the college's website is also important for faculty because many students ask us questions that they could easily find on the college's website. As a busy faculty member, I do not enjoy having to guide my students to the college web page they could have found on their own.

When you get to college, you will also find that most have an electronic learning management system. If you are not familiar, a LMS is a way of teaching, learning and delivering courses through the Internet (i.e. Moodle, Blackboard, and Canvas). If you took a fully online course, the only access to the course content you would have would be through an LMS because you'll never be meeting the professor face to face. Even though your courses will not be online, colleges use LMS's because they help deliver the content to students in a very organized way. You can take quizzes, view handouts, submit papers and tests, and get class announcements emailed to you, all on the LMS. They make our job as teachers much easier and give you as students more transparency and clarity in regard to what you have to do and when. Most will even consolidate your due dates for all your courses. In short, LMS's help the professor organize their courses and help students see and manage all their courses in an organized fashion.

I have three pieces of advice in regard to your college's LMS.

- ➤ **Don't be afraid of it.** You cannot give yourself a bad grade and you cannot un-enroll yourself from the course so experiment and play. Get to know your college's LMS backward and forward so you know how it works, know where things are, and know how to get the information you need. The more you play on there, the faster you will be when it counts. For example, I post my office hours on our LMS and when students email me and ask what my hours are, I guide them back to the LMS page, a page they should have seen prior to contacting me.

- ➤ **Timed quizzes or tests are often given via the LMS.** You need to get used to taking these without getting overly nervous about the timer that counts down on the screen. I give quizzes before every class so it assures me that all the students in my classes read before they walk in the door. Do not worry, if you read the material, you will have enough time to take your quizzes.

- ➤ **LMS's are available for your smartphone.** If you organize your life via your cell phone, this third piece of advice is for you. One of my students told me that she downloaded the LMS app to her phone, synced her account, and now receives notifications and reminders right on her phone. I thought this was a great idea!

Use Keystrokes

Since you will be writing a great deal in college, learning how to use keystrokes in place of using your mouse to do certain things can save you a substantial amount of time. When you press a combination of keys at the same time to complete a task, this is a keystroke. For example, if you hit Control and the letter B at the same time, you are telling Word to bold what you type. Control + S saves your document and Control + I italicizes what you type. Everything you can do with a mouse, you should be able to do with a keystroke. When you use some commands often (save, print, bold, underline, etc.), you want to be able to do these without taking your hands off the keyboard. Using keystrokes may save only a second or two but think about if you are writing two or three 10-page papers. You will save a lot of time over the course of a semester. Microsoft Word has a ton of them but you can also program your own keystrokes if you want to.

I grade all my papers digitally rather than having students hand in hard copies. I have ten of the most common comments I make on student papers keystroked so when I grade, I rarely have to take my hands off the keyboard. It saves me so much time. Like with other suggestions, I am not going to walk you through how to do this because it is your job. Just Google search your version of Word with the phrase 'keyboard shortcuts' and I guarantee it will save you time when you write anything for college and beyond.

Effective Time Management

While you will have free time, college work will keep you busy and if you are not busy, you may not be doing the work you need to do. Effective time management is so important for success in college and once you graduate and get a job. Here are some suggestions that I know can help.

Keep a Calendar

Keep a calendar. It is absolutely crucial for you to keep a calendar. What type of calendar is up to you but I absolutely cannot overstate the importance of doing it. Even if you are used to juggling several things at once, college will yield a different type of multi-tasking. You will have daily, weekly and monthly tasks, and tasks that will happen three months down the road (i.e. your term paper). Your different classes, homework for those classes, small and big papers, tests, friends, weekends, and sleep, will all take your time and attention. Without a way to organize what you do and when you do it, college will become more difficult to manage, especially given the fact that we as professors will not be nagging and reminding you about assignments. We assign papers then wait for them to come in on the due date and if they do not, they do not.

If your college uses Gmail as its email server, Google calendar is great. You can put everything in there with only a few clicks and you can tell it to repeat events each week. You can easily have Google send you an email or popup notification of an event minutes, hours, days or even weeks in advance. One of my students said that setting calendar notifications was the best thing she did for herself. You can put your classes, practices, meetings, due dates, lunch and even gym time into your calendar. If your school does not have an electronic calendar, either get a Gmail account or use a different calendar system that works for you. If you do this, you can also have it on your phone for easy access.

I keep a Google calendar for my classes, meetings and appointments. I keep it on a weekly view so I only see where I need to be for that week only. I use pop up notifications because I am so caught up in my work that I lose track of time. This system works great for me and while there may be a better system for you, the strong benefits of keeping a calendar are clear.

I also suggest getting a semester at a glance calendar. These calendars have the entire semester on one single page. Enter in all-important dates pertaining to your school assignments, such as term papers. Also, add all your athletic and family obligation dates. In short, put everything on the calendar that is important not to forget and post it in a very visible place where you do your work. I keep a semester at a glance calendar and I put in every single assignment that is coming for the entire semester for every class. I also color code each class to make it easier for me to see. I keep a copy on my computer desktop but I also have one on the wall right in front of my desk so it is always right in front of me.

Lastly, I think it's a smart move put in a regular appointment for your study time into the calendar in each day. If you dedicate a specific amount of time each day for homework, then you will be more likely to get it done. If you schedule in time every day and treat this time like a job, when the end of the semester comes and everyone is stressed about working late into the night, you will have free time to relax. You can schedule naps into your calendar too – rest is important!

Keep a To Do List

I am a list maker. I make lists of what to do at work, at home, and even for play. Personally, I make lists because I want to keep track of what I need to do but I also make them because it is satisfying to cross things off as I go. To keep it organized, I have made a two column by four-row table in my Word processor. I put each of my classes in their own cell. I also have individual cells for my committee and department work as well as a cell designated for my list of things to do at home. I save this to the top corner of my desktop and it opens up automatically every morning when I boot up my computer. I prioritize by shading in bright green my most important tasks for the day. As a new task arises, I immediately put it in its appropriate place on my 'to do' list. This way, I am able to keep track of everything that I need to do and in what particular order it needs to be done.

Once my list is done, I find it important to split up the larger tasks into smaller ones. Having to write a big term paper and seeing it stare at you from your list may not help you at all. In fact, it might deter you from starting because it is such a big task. So, break it up into smaller sections. For example, as I wrote this book, I did not have 'write the book' on my list. Instead, I only had the chapter I was drafting on my list and I even had that broken down into smaller sections. As I completed each small section, I marked it off as complete and that, in itself, was a sense of accomplishment.

By doing this, the task of writing becomes less daunting and more like slowly chipping away at smaller, very doable elements of your task. For a large paper, start by researching and perhaps only put that on your list until you've done what you consider to be enough initial research (tip: gather your research

169

materials all at the same time in the same setting rather than reading and taking notes on each individual source as you find them. This helps you get in the zone doing one singular task).

How you choose to keep your list is up to you but there are things you want to take into consideration. First, make sure your list is organized the way that is most convenient and functional for you. Second, print your list out and bring it to classes so you can add tasks the professor assigns. After classes, go home and type all your new assignments, and prioritize as necessary. Lastly, if the format of your calendar is not working (i.e. your phone), try a different method rather than stress over one that may not work for you. Being open to change allows you to find a better way.

Sabrina (a sophomore) uses a monthly calendar on a white board and color-codes her tasks with different markers. She finds great satisfaction crossing things off and it is right in front of her workspace. She always has a handle on what's due and what is coming. Rather than a 'to do' list, Sabrina carries a planner with her to every class and when assignments are given, she writes them in. Again, pick a method that works for you but just be sure to keep a list of some kind.

Keep Your Work Close

Your days will not always be jam packed with classes or activities and you will find yourself with spare time. If you are in your room, then you are likely to have your computer, books, and notes (hopefully one notebook for each class) close by so you can get some work done. That may not be the case if you are away from school or way across campus.

Keeping that in mind, carry some of your work with you so if you find yourself with time, you can sit and get some done. You may be in the doctor's office, on the bus with your team, in an airport traveling with your family or friends, or just waiting for your next class. The point is that many of us are caught in situations where we end up having to wait. If you do have the spare time when you are waiting, why not get a bit of work done?

I am not suggesting that you lug a backpack full of books and notes and your computer everywhere. Instead, bring a single book when you have reading to do. If you have some writing to do, bring your laptop or tablet. You have a great deal of free time in a week so why not use it. Google 'time management calculator' to see how much spare time you actually have in a week. I think you might be surprised.

Time Management and the Student Athlete

Student athletes are in a different position than those students who are not playing a sport. While athletes have less time and possibly less energy to get their work done, there is still enough time, trust me. Most athletic teams in college will mandate study time each week. While it might not be a lot, you need to take advantage of that dedicated study time. Also, it is imperative that student athletes schedule in their own study time. It is going to be very easy to go back to bed after a hard morning workout but losing that portion of the day will be problematic if it becomes a habit.

You also need to be thoughtful about how and when you schedule your courses as you progress toward your degree. It may not be that important during your first year, but as you move forward, you will be taking harder upper level courses that will take much more of your time. On the same token, your time will be much more limited when you are in season. You will have practice and games and will travel more. Speak with your advisor about organizing your schedule so you are not taking a very difficult class load during the season. Take a full load of classes but just do not take the two hard lab sciences or a research methods class.

Rebekah, a recent graduate who was a NCAA athlete said, "Going back to bed after a morning workout is a high possibility if your classes are evening or afternoon ones. Sometimes the classes you need are only offered at night. I would take a short nap after a morning workout, then wake up and get to work before classes and my late practices. However, after my first two years, my habits changed from napping after morning workouts to getting breakfast to fuel me for the rest of the day. I would then work on some stuff, go to class, and then possibly catch a nap in the afternoon. Some days I did nap and some days I didn't."

Remember, you are a student first and an athlete second. If athletics becomes first and your academics suffer, the coach may bench or you will not be at school because you could not keep your grades up.

It happens to many more athletes than you realize and while the resources will be there to help you succeed, you have to reach out and utilize them. College employees, especially faculty, have seen students succeed and fail and we know what works and what does not. You have seen that statement in this book several times so use us. Let us help. Lastly, you should know that if you are not doing your work or choosing to act out in class, we might put a call in to your coach. While you may not listen to us, you will start to after the coach hears about it.

Health, Socialization and Balance

Roommates

If you are like most college students, you will be placed with a roommate who you have not met before. Colleges work very hard to match up roommates based on their likes and dislikes. You will probably fill out some type of online housing survey. When you do, the residence life office will ask you questions about yourself and attempt to match you with a roommate you are compatible with. They may have even suggested that you contact each other prior to the start of the semester to get to know each other and decide what each of you is bringing for the room. Colleges succeed in this endeavor more times than they fail but there are failures.

So, what do you do if you find that you are not compatible with your roommate? It is unlikely that you will be able to switch rooms in the first semester so you will have to figure out a way to cope. You may be able to switch rooms after the first semester because some first year students will have dropped out. You want to work with your roommate rather than bide time because you do not want your home (your room) to become a place that feels uncomfortable.

This is not a counseling or conflict resolution book so I will not go on for pages speaking to dealing with conflict in a constructive way. I will say a few things though. First, completely listen to your roommate when they come to you with a conflict. Do not interrupt until they are done. Then, work to paraphrase back what you heard, ask questions, and listen to any clarification so you both are on exactly the same page. Respond accordingly without judging. Then work toward a solution. If you have a conflict,

173

then approach your roommate and ask that they follow this system as well. Not interrupting and paraphrasing back are both absolutely crucial and will allow you to really listen. It takes practice but give it a shot, and do not give up. There are many solid conflict resolution books out there and I would think that your college has a class or two on this subject. If they do, take it, because it can help you for life, not just with roommate issues. It is all about being able to communicate so learning how to do it better can always help!

With any conflict you have with anyone, be an adult and admit to the shortcomings that are yours. Take responsibility for your behaviors and your part in the conflict. Admission of responsibility with a 'but' afterwards is not an admission at all. Work towards adulthood and take credit for what is yours – good and bad.

As I have mentioned before, being in contact and working toward friendship before you even get to school can make this part of your transition so much easier. Whether it be on the phone, Skype, or in person, work to make this happen. You will be happy you did.

Your Time, Friends, and Extra Curricular Activities

You will make friends, trust me. Friends in college are great because you are all going through the same process of transition and that breeds similar experiences. It is also wonderful because you can express your feeling and issues to them and they can do the same. If you become known as a good listener, however, you may be the person who people come to for help. This is fine. It is wonderful to be there for your friends. Try not to judge while helping them find their own solutions without forcing your opinion on

174

them. Be a facilitator rather than an enabler. Most of all, learn to say no if you have to. If you have neither the time nor energy to help, then be honest and tell them. It does a disservice to them if you are not 'present' and a disservice to yourself because you are not doing what you need to do for you.

The same holds true for extracurricular activities such as student government, outdoor clubs, school co-ops and club athletic teams. It is great to be involved because you will make more connections and those your friendships will be stronger. Just use caution when thinking about your time. Be willing to say no using your academics as the reason. No one will get upset with you and if they do, it is *their* priorities that are likely in the wrong place. Be stingy with your time when you need to.

Your Health

You surely have heard of the freshman fifteen. If not, it is the amount of weight you might gain in your first year. The academic research on the subject (not Google search results) is limited but most say that more freshman gain weight than lose and men are more likely to gain weight than women are. That being said, the research also shows that the average freshman weight gain is about three pounds and that is put on during the first semester (Vadeboncoeur et al., 2015). Just be aware because weight gain may sneak up on you. This transition to college will be difficult and when struggling to cope, the heavy comfort food that will be served in your cafeteria can become problematic very quickly if eaten in large amounts.

With that in mind, I want to give some general advice on how to stay as healthy as you can when working through the transition of your first semester.

Know that a good diet will be helpful. Avoid overeating because the opportunity of endless cafeteria food is in front of you. Be regular with your eating and do not skip meals, especially breakfast. This will get you up a bit earlier for your morning class but your body will need the energy.

In your school's cafeteria, take only a plate to fill rather than a tray where more plates can be added. It may sound silly, but you are more likely to eat less without that tray. Avoid the heavy creamy options and opt for lean meats and salads. If your cafeteria has a 'cooked in front of you station,' take advantage because you know it is fresh and you know what is in the food you are about to eat. I am not a nutrition expert and there are many websites that can help you if you want more information. Suffice it to say that a little thoughtfulness on what you eat can go a long way.

Outside of the cafeteria, eat healthy snacks as much as possible (peanuts and peanut butter, fruit, etc.) and avoid those late night pizzas, subs, and wings as much as possible. I will be the first to admit that I was guilty of eating as much pizza, subs and wings as I could get my hands on when I was in college, so I come from a place of experience here. Because of this, note that I am not commanding you to eat healthy because that is not realistic. I would rather you be aware that weight gain might sneak up on you. Lastly, do not forget that alcohol is loaded with calories and the more you drink, the more weight you will gain. Just keep that in mind.

In relation to non-food related advice, there are other things you can do to stay healthy and have your body thank you. First, exercise regularly. While college athletes will have this taken care of, others will not, and walking, running, working out or taking a physical education class is important to consider. If you are wondering how much time you will have, trust me that

176

you will have enough time. Second, develop a regular sleep schedule and work to get up at the same time of the day regardless of whether you have a class or not. I am not saying you must wake up at 7:30am on a day that you do not have your 8:00am class. Instead, I am saying do not sleep until noon or later. Try to get up at 8:30 or as close to the time you get up on days when you have your morning classes.

Conclusion

The reason I am writing this book is that I want to give you the knowledge and skills that will give you an advantage toward college success. Any of the ideas that you can implement now, and in college, will help you succeed academically and in life. Please note that what I have advised in this and the previous chapter are techniques that will work but there are so many more ideas out there on the Internet and on your college's campus.

I hope that you visited the college's learning center when you toured the school. Even if you did not, you should, once you arrive on campus. My goal is to make you an effective and efficient student and I am excited to do that. I can only take you so far with this book and hopefully the tools I have offered will help you move in that direction. I also hope it will promote you to seek out more help and guidance once you get to school. The folks at your school are there to help but you need to find the right people. If all else fails, contact the director of your first year center and they will know where to send you.

I want to touch on one more point that I spoke about in Chapter 5. You need to balance and make time for yourself. You should work hard but you should also relax and not forget to enjoy life and the college atmosphere. Make sure you spend time doing things that alleviate stress for you. College, much like life, involves a balance. Work hard but relax. Do your homework and papers but make time for your friends and family. By implementing some of the things from the past three chapters, you will have more time to be able to make those work/play choices.

A Chapter for Students with Learning Differences

Introduction

The process of choosing a college can be a difficult one, especially if you do not have your heart set on a single college. The difficulty of finding the right college may be amplified if you have a learning difference or disability. You have to closely examine the range of services the college offers in relation to those learning differences. All colleges must comply with the Americans with Disabilities Act and provide reasonable access to services but make no mistake, not all colleges are created equal when it comes to the services they provide. Some may offer the minimum required by law and some may go well beyond what the law requires.

Before going further, I want to be clear about something. Regardless of your learning difference, you can absolutely succeed at college. The transition may be uncomfortable and difficult but once you get used to it and have your support system in place, you can succeed.

This chapter will focus on differentiating between college and high school in relation to students with learning differences. It will also help both you and your parents know what to look for, what questions to ask, and how to take advantage of the services offered by the college you attend. The theme that flows throughout this chapter is this: Unlike high school, colleges must only provide reasonable access to services, so the student needs to be their best advocate and seek out the services they need.

Learning Differences and the Law: IDEA vs. ADA

High School: Individuals With Disabilities Education Act (IDEA)

Up until a student with a learning difference graduates from high school, they are protected under the Individuals with Disabilities Education Act (IDEA). Without getting technical, IDEA stems from the No Child Left Behind Act and essentially states that K-12 schools must have procedures in place to push forward and graduate students who have a learning difference. The law promises that the student is going to be successful and graduate with whatever help is needed from the school. This is obviously a general statement but the premise about the core focus of the law is true.

Schools must come up with an individualized education plan (IEP) for each student. This plan must be reasonably calculated to enable a child to make progress in light of the child's circumstances. IDEA and specific IEP's do not promise any specific level of education and do not promise any specific educational outcome (i.e. graduate high school). In several cases that have come before them, the federal courts have found that no law could guarantee those educational outcomes for any child. Even with this in mind, IDEA requires that schools be very pro-active toward the student's success.

The reason this needs to be said focuses around the student's expectations. Students with a learning difference and their parents come to expect a certain level of attention and accommodation from the school, teachers and administrators. Parents are kept in the loop and are active participants and facilitators in helping their child move toward graduation with accommodations. IDEA is a law about successfully graduating high school and parents play a significant role advocating for their child. Unfortunately, parents and students may not experience that same level of proactive involvement in the college setting and the Americans with Disabilities Act does not require it.

College: Americans With Disabilities Act

Section 504 of the Rehabilitation Act is under the umbrella of the amended Americans with Disabilities Act (ADA). The original ADA law was less about *success* and more about *access*. Under the ADA, people with disabilities must be offered the same opportunities to participate in areas "including jobs, school, transportation and all public and private places that are open to the general public." (ADA National Network, n.d.) Denying these opportunities is considered discrimination and is prohibited. In short, the ADA demands that people with disabilities get equal opportunity.

When the ADA was formed, the law prohibited discrimination based on race, color, religion, or national origin. When it was amended, it enveloped Section 504 of the Rehabilitation Act of 1973 and applied to primary schools, secondary schools and colleges that receive federal funding (U.S. Department of Civil Rights, n.d.). The law requires these institutions to provide equal opportunity to education for those with disabilities. These include mental, physical and learning disabilities.

I have used the phrase 'equal opportunity' twice in the previous two paragraphs. This phrase is an important one to understand because it starkly differentiates the IDEA from the ADA and what is required of them. The ADA is a civil rights law and requires that colleges provide access to an equitable education. It does not require, or mandate however, that the college provide whatever is necessary for the student to graduate. It only requires reasonable access to the accommodations - and this is very different from what students and parents are familiar with.

The Importance of this Difference

Over the course of a student's education throughout high school, you and your parent(s) have come to have certain expectations about the level of accommodation you receive. In college, it is not the

182

same and this must be understood before you even begin to look at colleges. Here are the primary differences in relation to what the ADA offers you compared to the IDEA.

> ➤ **As a college student, you are no longer covered under IDEA and if eligible, are now covered under the ADA.**

> ➤ **Even if you were eligible under IDEA, you are not automatically eligible under the ADA.**

> ➤ **You have the right to access, not to success.** The college must have procedures in place to offer reasonable accommodations when asked to.

> ➤ **Reasonable accommodations does not equal all requested accommodations.** The college only needs to put a reasonable accommodation in place even if it is not the personal choice or preference of the student.

> ➤ **You are required to be pro-active and seek out accommodations for yourself.** The college will not seek you out nor do they have to.

Given these differences, the burden is on you to research the ADA and what it provides. The burden is also on you to research what colleges have to offer in regard to accommodations. Not all college are equal in the level of accommodations they provide. Some do what they have to do (the minimum) and some go well beyond. Remember, the IDEA guarantees success and the ADA guarantees access.

Getting Your Learning Difference Assessed

A college is required to do nothing extra for you unless you have current official documentation (usually within five years) confirming that you have a learning difference. The documentation is proof that you have a learning difference and guides the college in deciding what accommodations they need to offer you. Once the college has that official documentation, they will use Section 504 of the Rehabilitation Act of 1973 to guide accommodations. Section 504 basically says that a school cannot discriminate against you if you have a disability. You must be assessed to determine if you qualify for those reasonable accommodations.

Being assessed is important and while the law does allow colleges to do their own assessment, it is strongly advised that you get a new or renewed medical assessment prior to going off to college. Testing and getting results takes time. You may wait several weeks for your testing to be done and results to come back. In short, you want to be able to walk into your college's disability resources office the day you get to school and have your accommodations in place on the first day of classes.

The intrusiveness and time spent at the testing itself will vary based on the degree of disability but it is likely to last a few days. It can cost anywhere from $500 to $5,000, again depending on the degree of disability. Some insurance companies will cover the cost of the testing but you or your parents should find out prior to making the appointment.

Suggestions

Suggestions When Researching/Visiting Colleges

All students headed to college need to do their research so they can make an informed choice about which college is the right one for them. Students with learning differences have to take that research one-step further. They should assess the strength of each college's disability resources office, staff, and available accommodations. As I noted above, not all schools are created equal and the law only requires the college provide the minimum level of reasonable accommodations. For example, some colleges offer smart pens or recorders while others have designated note takers in addition to the recording device. You will not know what they offer until you ask the questions that you need to.

When researching online, find the phone number and call each college's disability resources office (names will vary among colleges). Speak to a staff member or the coordinator and ask about:

➢ **The most recent list of available accommodations the college offers.**

➢ **If there are specific accommodations that are beneficial to you, ask if they can or will work with you to implement them.** If they say no, it does not mean they are not worth pursuing as a college because they may have accommodations that are even more beneficial than the one specific to you.

➢ **Ask what documentation you need to have.**

➢ **Ask how recent that documentation needs to be.**

➢ **Ask about what their procedures are to get accommodations.**

➢ **Ask the disability resources coordinator if the professors are easy to work with.**

Make sure you take notes on each college but it might also be smart to make a graph with each college on the top row and each accommodation offered in separate columns. Then you can simply put a check mark in when you find out if the college offers that specific accommodation. Please take note that the advice I am giving is for you to make that call and for you to do the research rather than your parents. Here, there are two distinct benefits. First and as noted throughout the book, it is your education and you need to begin to take charge. Second, the sooner *you* can make a connection with the disability resources coordinator or staff member, the easier your transition will be when you choose that college.

When you visit each college, go to the disability resources office with your research about the college's level of accommodations in hand. Introduce yourself to the staff to continue making those connections. Remember the names of the staff members you speak to and ask for the same one(s) each time you call and when you visit. You will want to confirm that your list of most recent accommodations is correct and that the college's procedures to obtain accommodations are still the same. I would suggest bringing a copy of your testing results and then begin to talk about what a potential plan for you would look like. While parental input at the onset is acceptable, you should work to start facilitating your own accommodations the best that you can. Moreover, parents can make suggestions as to what accommodations might be beneficial but it is solely up to the college's disability resources office to decide what accommodations they will offer you. When preparing for that meeting, you may want to practice your conversation with someone first, video record yourself, or practice in front of a mirror. It can only help prepare you for your meeting.

Once you have made your decision and have committed to a specific college, there are two things you should absolutely do. You should re-contact the disability resources office and officially submit your assessment results so your accommodations can be official before you head off to school in August. This also gives you the opportunity to communicate your thoughts regarding the plan and any changes you might consider being beneficial. You should also write a letter or email to your professors introducing yourself and inform them that you have a learning difference and you will have accommodations. Do not order them to comply and make sure you are respectful. Also, make it clear that you are excited about their class and that you just wanted to let them know. Doing this has the same benefits as communicating with the office staff, but it goes further. Your professors are the ones you are going to see all week so beginning a dialog and making that connection can never hurt. Note: Do not despair if they do not respond right away (or at all) because many of us scatter in the summer and some do not check their email that often or at all.

Suggestions For When You Arrive at Your School

You know what is coming in the next sentence. The first thing you need to do is go back to the disability resources office, reconnect, and make sure your accommodations are in place. Also, get any paperwork you need so you can officially inform your professors of your accommodations. Then go meet each of your professors, give them the paperwork (if that is the procedure) and start a conversation with them. Things will be a bit hectic for professors the first week of classes so the best time to catch them is during their office hours. Seeing them in person in their office is very important so you can make that initial connection.

Suggestions to Work on Throughout your First Semester and Beyond

As I have said in many places in this book, every college student's experience is different. Students have to find what works for them in a variety of different places (i.e. classes, studying). The same holds true for students with learning differences. You need to figure out how you want to manage the accommodations you will receive and how you set up your own processes that will help you succeed. Below you will find some suggestions that could be helpful. Please note that I am not a psychiatrist but I have spent a great deal of time working with students with learning differences and disabilities resource offices. I have seen these suggestions work but as always, I encourage you to find the ones that work for you.

a. Develop Routines

Work Hard to Find Your Routines and Stick to Them

For anyone, developing a routine helps train the mind and body to know what to expect and when. You brush your teeth in the same way with the same hand every morning because you have developed a routine. Could you brush your teeth with your other hand? Of course. Try it. You will be successful but it will feel very strange to use your opposite hand. The same holds true for college, especially when you are likely going through the biggest transition of your life. Routines can include making or going to breakfast, picking out clothes the night before, or packing your backpack before you go to bed, among many others. As silly as it sounds, finding and maintaining routines from the minute you get to school can help reduce some of the transition stress fairly quickly. This advice works for all students but for some, especially those on the autism spectrum, routines become even more important.

Practice Transitioning From One Activity to Another

In high school, your routine is set out for you and it is very similar from one day to the next. College is not like this. You may have a 10:00am class two days a week, a 2:00pm class two days a week and a 7:00pm class once a week. Classes may be back-to-back or may

189

have large breaks between them. This makes it easy to lose track of when and where you need to be. It also makes it difficult to practice before you get to college because the routine is so much different in high school.

In relation to transitioning between activities, you can practice two things before you come to college. First, you can practice (consciously) getting out of your specific routine and getting an idea of what that discomfort feels like. Knowing how that discomfort feels can prepare you for the time when you are transitioning from activity to activity. For example, eat something different at a different time or walk down a hallway at school that you normally would not when headed to class.

Second, use your technology. If you use an electronic calendar such as the one provided by Google, it would be helpful. You can set up all the activities you have to do. More importantly, you can set up notifications for each event and if you have an event that repeats all semester (i.e. classes, breakfast, physical activity), Google calendar notifications will repeat as well. These notifications include pop-ups and email, and you can set them up to notify you ahead of time. Any technological assistance you can give yourself will be helpful and as always, find what works for you

Put on Your Schedule to Check Your Schedule

When you wake up in the morning, start a routine of checking your schedule for the day. Make a repeating calendar entry that tells you to check your schedule for the day. Then check your schedule and continue to check as many times in the day as you need to. Just do not forget to turn your phone on silent when in class so the audible notifications will not interrupt the class and professor.

Make Use of Assistive Technologies

Speak to the disability resources office and find out what assistive technologies they have available (i.e. smart pens, speech-to-text converters). Start experimenting with them. While high schools may have used some assistive technologies, colleges may have a wider array of tools you can use that can help you succeed. Since you have likely been using some technology, you know what can work for you but do not let that stop you from experimenting with other technologies. There may be different technologies that will work better for you if you just try them. Also, there are websites available for trying out and practicing with technology (i.e. Kurzweil, Jaws, Dragon, Smart pen). I actually used a text to speech converter to help proof this book. A note of caution though, try different technologies early in the semester when you are not so busy. Do not try them when you are stressed out and have a ton of work to do

191

because that may bring in additional and unneeded anxiety.

Work on Social Communication

In college, you will learn how to express and support your views without it having to become a personal attack in class. You will learn how to professionally communicate with faculty and other students. Even if your parents have been the primary ones to advocate for you, college will prepare you to advocate for yourself. You will also learn to communicate with other students in social situations and in situations where there is conflict. All of these types of communication are as important to work on as your academics.

I am not a psychologist nor do I assert that I am an expert in social communication techniques. That being said, I do know that any type of communication takes practice and feedback on that practice. In the residence halls and with your friends, you can certainly ask for feedback in relation to whether you are communicating in a way that is functional to that relationship. You can also do that with professors. Asking is always the key. There is a great deal of additional information in books and on the web so please avail yourself of them.

Testing Accommodations

The ADA guarantees that you will receive testing accommodations that are relevant to your learning difference. Just because you get them does not mean you should always use them. For example, if you get extra time on a test, I would strongly suggest you try to finish it in the regular allotted time and then take the extra time if you need it. If a professor has three or four exams, you also can try to reduce the amount of time with each successive test.

I want you to succeed and if you need all or some of that extra time, you should absolutely take it. If you can do it in the regular time, however, you should try as hard as you can to do so. The reason I say this is that once you're out of school in and a work situation, your boss may be less likely to give you extra time on tasks that they need done immediately. Part of college is training students to become functioning members of society who can assimilate directly into successful full time employment. This is just one way you can be better prepared in your future jobs.

General Academic Advice

First off, speaking to your professors often about where you stand in their class and how you are doing is more beneficial than I can describe. Our job as teachers is just as relevant outside the classroom as inside. Professors are there to help guide you toward knowledge and adulthood so use them as a resource as much as you need to. While not all professors want to mentor outside the class, you can learn a great deal from those that do and their willingness should be obvious right from the start.

Try not to shy away from classes that have activities that make you uncomfortable. If possible, you want to be able to confront your fears as much as you can, even if that makes you uncomfortable. The classroom may not be the first place that you want to confront fears (i.e. public presentations, group work) but it is a great place to take some of those fears and work on moving beyond them. There is a good chance you will have to make presentations in courses when you are in college, especially in your upper level courses. Perhaps start working on them in a club or other another extra-curricular activity and then take what you have learned from there into the classroom.

In class, sit near the front and record the lectures. Sitting in the front inherently leads to you paying more attention. One reason is that you cannot see everything that the students behind you are doing. They are hopefully listening and taking notes but the less visual stimuli you have, the better.

A Final Note on This Transition

You will be in the same boat as every other incoming first year college student. For most, it will be the biggest transition of your life and that cannot be understated. All this means is that you have to pay attention and know that it is going to be a significant change in your life. We want you to work to seek success in ways that are best for you. We want you to be independent but we also want you to feel comfortable asking for help. Whether it is study skills or doing your own laundry, work to be independent but ask for help if it is scary or uncomfortable.

My two decades of experience in a college known for being receptive to students with learning differences leads me to this final advice. Do not change your medications right before college and certainly do not stop taking them. Also, it will likely be a mistake to drop your counselor if you have one. Stick with the one you have or get a new one near your college because they are trained professionals and can help ease the transition.

Conclusion

There is much more advice I could give you about success but these suggestions are the ones that are most relevant and important to professors. A learning difference is just that, a difference. You can succeed and excel at college and much of your success will revolve around you being as comfortable as you can be. Be your best advocate.

You can work to prepare yourself for college but it is ok to be nervous because all first year students are, even if they do not show it. Moreover, your learning difference is only an obstacle to success. You absolutely can succeed and as professors, we want that and will help.

A Chapter for Parents

Introduction

This chapter is written for you but it is also written to allow your parents the ability to help you succeed in college. As you might guess, it is not a matter of your parents helping you with work or administrative tasks. It is about your parents giving you the room to grow as an adult and as a college student. Both parents and students can benefit from this chapter because you can be on the same page and have the same expectations. While this chapter focuses on advice from a professor's perspective, many websites out there can also be helpful.

Advice for Student and Parents

This is a Transition for Both of You

Student: I know that by now you are sick of me saying that it is a transition for you and while I am going to say it here too, I am going to put it into a different context. One of the ways that the transition from high school to college becomes apparent is the change in your relationship with your parents. They may be your best friend or your worst enemy but you have lived under their roof for eighteen years and that is going to change. There will be no curfews, no restrictions, no getting grounded and no fights about things going on at home. Sounds great, right? Well, you're also losing out on dinner, getting your laundry done or your room cleaned, getting money if you need it, rides, emotional support and help with school, just to name a few. What I am trying to say is that the transition is not just being at college but also being away from the home environment, which is likely all you have ever known.

You probably can predict my response to this. First, learn to live on your own and do all the tasks that you need to do. Homework and classwork, of course but you also want to be able to make your own appointments, go to the doctor if you need it, get a bank account and do other administrative tasks that your parents might have done for you. You want to help them help you by making sure that you are doing what you need to be doing without relying on them. Some parents might be all right with loosening the reigns. However, some parents will want to continue to take care of you and you need to gently assert that you can take care of yourself and be an adult. While you are still in high school, you can show them that you can take care of yourself in college by doing some of

198

the things I have listed above. You are on a move toward adulthood, which means that you have to show them that you can handle independence.

Parent: If this is your first college-bound child, it is likely going to be tough. Some of you will be incredibly nervous about your child leaving home. The difficulty could be about academics, experiences with drugs or alcohol, late nights, not studying, or just the fact that they will not be around the way they have been for eighteen years. I do not want to underestimate or minimize what you are feeling but I do want you to understand that this is a seminal point in your child's life. It is their big moment. Your child is starting (right now) their journey into adulthood and you can help them. Help them by letting them start their journey. Be sad that they are gone but give them the space. Let them do the things that you would normally do for them. Let them make their appointments and get their homework done. Let them do their own laundry when they come home. Let them realize the consequences of their actions whether it be class related or student conduct related. I am not asserting that you should not support them but I am asserting that you let them take the lead. They are going to have to do it when they graduate college so why not let them start their transition now. You would be doing them a disservice if you hovered and let them postpone adulthood.

On the other hand, you may be thrilled. Some of you will feel that excitement and a strong sense of accomplishment that you raised a child who is now going off to college. If this is the case then I am extremely happy for you!

Before Going Off to College

Student: If you want to look into buying your books so you can get started reading, just contact your professors or the college bookstore. You should be able to get the information you need to get working. Also, start thinking about what the college needs from you before you get there. Are there any forms, documents, or immunizations they need? If so, work to get them yourself. Get your own bank account. Pack a role of duct tape and perhaps a small tool kit. Just pack early and enjoy summer. You deserve it!

Parent: I think the best advice I can give here is about the conversations you should be having with your child over the course of the summer. Some of these conversations could be tough and uncomfortable. You need to talk about money. Will you be giving them money while they are in college and if so, how much and how often? Are there things you do not want your money paying for? Are there other restrictions you want to put on them in regard to money? It is simply better to have the conversation now rather than in a crisis situation later. Set expectations early and stick to your guns.

You absolutely must have the conversation about accountability and responsibility. You absolutely must have the conversation about sexual assault and consent (you should read the sections of the college's student handbook on drugs alcohol, and sexual assault). Let them know that you can be of support to them but you cannot bail them out. They need to know that they will be held accountable for their actions in and out of class. Many will have their first experiences with sex, drugs and alcohol while in college. They may not partake but they will see their fair share of it and there is little you can really do about it. Now is the time to instill common sense into them by telling them that their actions have consequences.

Drop Off Day

Student: Drop off day is a significant event in a parent's life. Whether you are the first child to go to college or the last, it signifies a radical change in life for everyone. I strongly believe that parents have the right to be emotional when dropping off their son or daughter. I also think it is less relevant that this may be embarrassing to you. Students, you have to give your parent's something here. You need to allow them to be sad and to hug on you more than you think is necessary – just deal with it. They have strong feelings and those feelings are going to be different from yours. Moreover, you are not going to be the only one with emotional parents and if the goal is to make a good first impression or be cool in front of your residence hall mates, then deal with that too. They are probably going through the same thing that you are going through with your parents and the whole move-in day process will be all forgotten by the next morning. This is a significant transition for them as much as it is for you and you need to recognize that and be ok with their emotion.

Oh yes, do not forget to eat and drink lots of water. It could be quite hot and you could be climbing many stairs!

Parent: Drop off day is a significant event in your child's life. Whether it is the first child to go to college or the last, it signifies a radical change in life for everyone. While it will likely be a sad day for you, it might be better for your child if you hold back those emotions a bit. I am not suggesting that you do not show any emotion or sadness, but if you find yourself becoming overly emotional, it might have an impact on your child. Transition will be very difficult for them although they may not show it.

You may embarrass them but more importantly, it might make them start down a road toward homesickness and that can make it more difficult for them. Be emotional but if possible, be less outwardly emotional. Get some pictures and hugs, help them get their things into their room, and let them do the rest (i.e. make friends, unpack and decorate their room). You will see them soon enough and they need to have the time to settle in and begin to make connections.

Tell them what you think is going to be important for them to hear as they are starting down that adulthood role. Hint: you should not be telling them to brush their teeth or do their homework. When my parents dropped me off at my first college, my father said one simple thing to me that has stuck with me to this day. He said, "Make me proud" and while I may not have been the best college student in the beginning, I came around.

Do not forget to eat and drink a lot of water.

Coming Home

Student: You might find yourself homesick and wanting to go home for the comfort of your own bed, your house, your parents, your pet(s) and a home cooked meal or two. Even if you are attending a college close to home, you will want to avoid going home within the first month. Perhaps even wait until you have a few days off for fall break. It might be tough and you may feel like you need the comfort of home but I strongly urge you to fight through it and to stay at school.

As I have mentioned throughout this book, it is incredibly important to make connections right when you arrive at school. Not only will it make the academic transition easier, it will make the social transition easier as well. The more you socialize and the more friends you make early on, the less homesick you will be. So, staying has a dual purpose. On one hand, it allows you to make friends and on the other, it allows you to feel less of a need to go home. While your parents may not be happy about this, those first few weeks of school are the transformative ones and you need to be there both during the week and during the weekends.

On the same note, work to not go home during the last four weeks of the semester, except for holidays like Thanksgiving. As I have spoken about before, you are going to be very busy and it will only put you behind if you go home during that time. The final third of the semester is definitely not the time to fall behind. If you think you are going to do work when you are home, you will not at all or you will get about 20% of what you would be done if you were at school. Stay focused and finish strong.

Parent: Even if you are feeling the benefits of the long awaited empty nest, you will miss your child once they are away at college. It is as much of a transition for you as it is for them, albeit a different one. You have helped, nudged, and raised your child get to this point but now it is time for them to move into adulthood.

This movement into independence starts now and as such, it would be smart to let them have this time to begin the transition on their own. As such, discourage or do not let your child come home often, certainly not in the first four weeks or the last four weeks. They need to be involved with other students, especially on the weekend. It is so incredibly important for them to make connections at college in the first few weeks. These can be with other students, faculty and staff. Whatever connections they make early on can have a significant impact on both their success and longevity at college. If you are going to visit, do so during family weekend which is usually in the fall semester (just make your hotel reservations early).

In relation to connections with other students, they need to experience the social life that takes place mainly on the weekends. It is not a matter of promoting alcohol or drug use but instead allowing them the time to grow as an adult, make adult decisions and gain friendships. Encouraging them to come home early or often makes it more difficult to make friendships in the end. Asking them to come home often can increase homesickness when they are at school. Coping with the transition is an important part of their first year of college and encouraging frequent and early visits home can do more harm than good.

A Parent's Involvement in Academics and Administration

Just this year, I had the parent of a college junior call me about getting her child into one of my courses that was at maximum capacity. I initially thought she was the student that was trying to get into the class but once I spoke with her, I realized that it was her child that was seeking entry. As I always do, I told her that her child needed to contact me and make her case. Once I indicated that, I said my goodbyes and waited for her child to call me (who never did, by the way). In another case, a parent called me around mid-semester after her first year child missed two scheduled appointments with me. She explained that he was not very good at administrative work so she was doing it for him. While she was not initially happy about it, I told her that he was not very good at that work because she was doing it for him. I simply would not let her do that work. It was tough to hear but she understood and allowed her child to take the reins, which he finally did.

Student: This is your time to be an adult and make adult decisions (including mistakes). Since this is likely your first venture into independence, it is crucially important to embrace that independence and make your college experience your own. In other words, you run the show. Your parents may want to help and if they do, understand that it is coming from a place of good intentions. That being said, it will do you more harm than good to let your parents take the lead with your administrative tasks. You cannot be independent if your parents are doing work for you making appointments, checking on your grades, etc. You are the only one that should call or email professors about issues you are having or administrative tasks you need to take care of. This may sound harsh but by letting your parents do this work, you only embarrass yourself in front of your professors and your growth as an adult will not progress as it should.

Parent: I fully understand how difficult this transition is for you, especially if it is your first child. You want to be protective and you want to help your child succeed. It is completely normal and you are certainly not alone with these feelings.

So many parents take full control at the application, college and orientation stages, which I strongly discourage. Many parents feel that they must complete the administrative work for their college-bound child. You should not do it during the college search and you should not do it once they arrive at college.

We live in a society that has changed, especially in relation to our children. We have become very protective and play a much more significant role in our children's lives. In short, the research shows that in this day and age, children feel privileged. Proper or improper, these feelings of privilege create significant problems in college education because they may not have experienced losing, getting a bad grade, or they have been taught that the effort is just as important as the product, which is not true in college. This creates stress for both the students and faculty because as faculty, we can only see their product.

Unfortunately, you will do a disservice to your child if you are a 'helicopter parent.' You will always be their parent but they need to experience the successes and failures that college will bring. I am fully aware that I am being repetitive but they need to succeed in classes without you and they need to fail in classes without you. Do not volunteer to edit or proof papers and always encourage them to see their professor or advisor if a problem comes up. Do not call the professor because we are not allowed to talk with you without your child's consent. The law prevents me from speaking to you without a FERPA waiver but even if I had one, I will only speak to you if your child is present.

I can say it plainly: If your child's success hinges around your help, how will that prepare them for their first job or marriage or their first child? It likely will not. They need to learn how to do these tasks like we all did when we were in college. I cannot put enough stress on this statement. Be there to support them but let them find the path themselves.

Communication

Student: You are going to get busy and you are going to make friends. You will have schoolwork to do and you are going to be socializing. You will be staying up late, going to practice and studying. In short, you are going to find yourself busy and excited in your new surroundings. You may end up not talking to your parents very much.

While I will not tell you how much you should talk to your parents, I will say that you need to set up some type of schedule and mode of communication. Just because you are out of the house does not mean that they are not thinking about you and not worried about you. Work with them to figure out how often you plan on talking and the mode of communication that works for *both* of you. If you need to set a day of the week and a specific time, do so. It's fine if you do not need to be that specific, but it will be important for you to make the time to keep your parents in the loop.

Parents: You want to work with your college bound student to make a plan together on how to communicate. The plan is crucial because it sets standards and you both know what is expected of you.

You may end up finding that your child does not stick with the schedule or is not communicating with you enough. They may also not be as forthcoming with you about the important things that are going on with them. While I hope this does not happen, you may end up feeling a bit shut out. I am not a psychiatrist so all I can recommend is to be patient and work hard to keep the communication lines open as best you can.

I do want to briefly focus on when you feel your child may be having serious issues with mental health, alcohol or drugs. No one wants to see his or her children in a bad place. Be a good parent but a prudent one as well. If your child is struggling, a good starting point is to call the Dean of Students or Campus Life office. They have a great deal of experience in this realm and have many options at their disposal to help.

Conclusion

Student and Parents: Congratulations! You did it! Congratulations to all of you. This is such an exciting time and a child going off to college means that you all succeeded! I love being on campus during drop off day and during family weekend because I get to see families and not just students. To see families connect on that first day and reconnect when parents come and visit is so gratifying. With my whole heart, I want to sincerely and excitedly congratulate all of you!

Final Thoughts

College is a big deal! Only about one of three adults have bachelor's degrees so it is a great accomplishment. You have made the commitment to go and now you just have to start the work to find the right school for you. It is out there, I promise. Once you get there, just do your job.

My goal was to give you advice that you can use and I hope I have done that. Go get it and again, congratulations!!

References

ADA National Network (n.d.). What is the Americans with Disabilities Act (ADA)? Retrieved January 15, 2017 from https://adata.org/learn-about-ada.

American School and University. (n.d.). Colleges with the most acreage. Retrieved February 15, 2016, from http://asumag.com/top-10s/colleges-most-acreage.

Boost eLearning. (2015, July 1). Google Apps for Education Anticipated to Reach 110 Million Users by 2020. Retrieved August 03, 2016, from http://www.prnewswire.com/news-releases/google-apps-for-education-anticipated-to-reach-110-million-users-by-2020-300107878.html

Brown, B. (2012, June 5). Wellesley High grads told: "You're not special". Retrieved June 29, 2015, from http://theswelleslyreport.com/2012/06/wellesley-high-grads-told-youre-not-special/.

Carter, (R. 2013). What is the 20-year trend on faculty with doctorate degrees? Retrieved August 26, 2017, from http://jcsu.edu/home/ask-dr/questions-and-answers/what-is-the-20-year-trend-on-faculty-with-doctorate-degrees.

Eagan, Kevin, Ella Bara Stolzenberg, Joseph J. Ramirez, Melissa C. Aragon, Maria Ramirez Suchard, and Sylvia Hurtado. (2014). The American Freshman: National Norms Fall 2014. Los Angeles: Higher Education Research Institute.

FinAid (2015). Student Loan Debt Clock. Retrieved May 29, 2015 from http://www.finaid.org/loans/studentloandebtclock.phtml.

Freidman, J. (2016, September 22). 10 Universities With the Most Undergraduate Students. Retrieved July 12, 2016, from http://www.usnews.com/education/best-colleges/the-short-list-college/articles/2016-09-22/10-universities-with-the-most-undergraduate-students.

Lardinois, F. (2017, January 24). Google says its G Suite for Education now has 70M users. Retrieved August 22, 2017, from https://techcrunch.com/2017/01/24/google-says-its-g-suite-for-education-now-has-70m-users/.

National Student Clearinghouse Research Center (2014, August 9) Report: Snapshot Report – Persistence-Retention. Retrieved June 8, 2015, from http://nscresearchcenter.org/snapshotreport-persistenceretention14/#prettyPhoto.

NCAA. (2016). Probability of Competing Beyond High School. Retrieved November 12, 2016, from http://www.ncaa.org/about/resources/research/probability-competing-beyond-high-school.

Pullaro Davis, N. (2015). Demand Drives Discount Rates. Retrieved June 8, 2015, from http://www.nacubo.org/Business_Officer_Magazine/Magazine_Archives/June_2013/Demand_Drives_Discount_Rates.html.

Shaffer, Suzanne (2014). What to Expect from College Orientation. Retrieved March 14, 2015 from https://www.teenlife.com/blogs/what-expect-college-orientation.

Smith-Barrow, D. (2016, January 5). Colleges Where Freshmen Usually Return: More than 97 percent of freshmen at each of these schools returned for another year. Retrieved December 5, 2016 from https://www.usnews.com/education/best-colleges/the-short-list-college/articles/2016-01-05/colleges-where-freshmen-usually-return.

U.S. Census Bureau (2015). Educational Attainment in the United States: 2014. Retrieved August 7, 2015 from http://www.census.gov/hhes/socdemo/education/data/cps/2014/tables.html.

U.S. Department of Civil Rights, n.d.). Information and Technical Assistance on the Americans with Disabilities Act. Retrieved September 16, 2017 from https://www.ada.gov/ada_intro.htm.

Vadeboncoeur, C, Townsend, N, and Foster, C. (2015). A meta-analysis of weight gain in first year university students: Is freshman 15 a myth? Retrieved August 09, 2016, from http://bmcobes.biomedcentral.com/articles/10.1186/s40608-015-0051-7.

About the Author

Will Pizio is a Professor of Criminal Justice at a small liberal arts college in the southeastern United States. He has been teaching criminal justice at that school for nineteen years but has taught in higher education for over twenty-three years. During this time, he has taught several first year seminar courses and was the Director of his college's First Year Center. Prior to teaching at the college level, he was a Trooper for the New York State Police for six years.

He received his Ph.D. in Criminal Justice from the State University of New York at Albany and more recently, he obtained a Master's degree in Cyber security from Utica College. He is currently the Director of the Graduate Criminal Justice program at his college.

He currently qualifies for the label 'aging hippie' and lives near Greensboro, North Carolina in a log cabin in the woods with his wife, dogs, cats, chickens and donkeys. Yes, donkeys!

CPSIA information can be obtained
at www.ICGtesting.com
Printed in the USA
FFOW03n0357200118
44503181-44331FF

9 781946 908919